VEGETARIAN MAGIC

AT THE REGENCY HOUSE SPA

Created and presented by

Chef John B. Nowakowski

Book Publishing Company
Summertown, Tennessee

Cover art and design: Estelle Carol
Interior photos: Vinnie Chiarelli
Food stylist: Dan Folleso
Illustrations: Kim Trainor
Interior design: Warren Jefferson

Printed in Canada by
Book Publishing Company
P.O. Box 99
Summertown, TN 38483
1-888-260-8458
www.bookpubco.com

10 09 08 07 06 05 04   9 8 7 6 5 4 3 2

Nowakowski, John B.
    Vegetarian magic at the Regency House Spa / created by John B. Nowakowski.
        p. cm.
    Includes index.
    ISBN 1-57067-100-1
        1. Vegetarian cookery. 2. Regency House Spa. I. Regency House Spa. II. Title.
    TX837 .N59 2000
    641.5'636--dc21   00-037853

Calculations for the nutritional analyses in this book are based on the average number of servings listed with the recipes and the average amount of an ingredient if a range is called for. Calculations are rounded up to the nearest gram. If two options for an ingredient are listed, the first one is used. Not included are fat used for frying (unless the amount is specified in the recipe), optional ingredients, or serving suggestions.

CONTENTS

DEDICATION

To my parents, Ann and John A. Nowakowski. Without their love, support, and guidance, I would not have been able to achieve so many exciting accomplishments in my life. To little John Christopher, you have completed me.

In memory of Dale Jean Peckham, my dear friend and good luck charm, thank you for always being there. We miss you dearly.

Special Thanks

To all of the wonderful guests at the Regency House Health Spa, your requests for our recipes and your true appreciation for what we have accomplished at the spa were a constant motivating factor in the creation of this book.

To the entire staff at Book Publishing Company for your commitment to excellence, especially Bob Holzapfel for believing in this project and mission for promoting good health. Special thanks to Cynthia Holzapfel, Michael Cook, and Warren Jefferson for your hard work in assembling the book.

To Nick Dejnega, without your support this would have never been possible.

Special thanks to Dr. Frank Sabatino. Your enthusiastic support, guidance, and education has enabled me to take this cuisine to the next level.

To Vinnie Chiarelli, without your photography expertise, this could not have been possible.

To Dan Folleso, food stylist, your attention to detail is second to none.

To Ilse Gotsch and Rita Ringler, for your passion for perfection in proofreading.

To Julio DiIorio, my recipe taste analyzer, confidant, marketing and design extraordinaire. We really miss you.

To my sous chefs Lance Cohen, Andrew Stanchak, and Andriana Lucoiu for your unending dedication to the cause. Thanks for "making it fun."

To Chefs Ken Hubscher and Debbie Fisher, for their delicious recipe contributions which made this endeavor more complete.

And finally, to my kitchen staff, who endured all of the changes that were necessary to create this exciting "Gourmet Vegetarian Cuisine" at the Spa.

John B. Nowakowski

John B. Nowakowski

FOREWORD

Faulty nutrition plays a major role in causing the chronic diseases (heart disease, arthritis, diabetes, cancer) that plague our society. We are a population addicted to salt, refined sugar, saturated fat, and disease-laden animal products. Over the last century, eating trends in the U.S. have increased these negative nutritional products in our diets, producing devastating health consequences. The drive to reduce these excesses and move toward a vegan/vegetarian approach (eliminating all animal and dairy products) is a direction that is timely and essential. The dramatic reduction and/or elimination of animal proteins, fats, and refined carbohydrates while increasing fiber-rich complex carbohydrates, vegetable-based proteins, fruits, and vegetables provides us with benefits that are continually reinforced by the best clinical and scientific information available.

However, our imaginations and choices are limited by the old ways we have been conditioned to do things. Even our sense of taste and our appreciation of wholesome natural foods has been jaded and shortchanged by the refined and processed foods we are used to. So, any new approach often elicits feelings of threat and disturbance. But with little patience and a small sense of adventure, new nutritional possibilities can open up and transform your life.

At the Regency House Spa, vegan nutrition is a crucial and powerful mainstay of our healthy living approach to healthcare. I am fortunate as a hygienic physician to work with a kitchen under the direction of Chef John Nowakowski. Chef John's extensive experience in food preparation encompasses the most innovative vegan approach that I have ever experienced in 20 years of nutritional practice in vegetarian health centers. Vibrant vegetarian nutrition involves so much of the energy of taste, colors, aromas, and presentation. Chef John will take you on a culinary adventure using nature's bounty as a palette to paint artistic displays that excite the palate, eye, and nose as well as nurture the body.

Because of our addiction to salt, sugar, and fat, people changing over to low-fat vegetarian cuisine often complain about the blandness of wholesome vegan recipes. Chef John has truly solved this dilemma by combining a masterful use of whole vegetarian foods with a tasteful use of gentle herbs and spices. His recipes entertain and delight both the novice and long-term vegetarian alike, making the transition to better nutrition exciting and easy. His recipes are time-tested, representing many hours of love and practice on thousands of spa guests, and will translate beautifully into your home kitchen environment.

Good nutrition isn't about deprivation or necessarily eating less. It's about eating well. So, embrace this fabulous opportunity to share Chef John's love and passion for food preparation, and let it lead you into the exciting world of vegan/vegetarian cuisine. The vitality and pleasure will be all yours. Bon Appetit.

Dr. Frank Sabatino

Dr. Frank Sabatino
Health Director—Regency House Natural Health Spa

INTRODUCTION

Everyone wants to know what has motivated me to take on the challenge of a vegan cookbook. Vegan cuisine is a lifestyle of the present and will provide ourselves and our children with a healthy, happier future. After spending the last 15 years in the high-pressured world of hotels and resorts as an executive chef, I also felt that a dietary and lifestyle change was necessary for me to enjoy a healthier life.

There are many wonderful vegetarian cookbooks available today. It seems like there is a new one coming out each month and for good reason. Surveys have shown that in the last 10 years, over 12 million Americans have taken on some form of a vegetarian lifestyle. With that taking place comes the ever-increasing demand for continuing education about this lifestyle.

It is now possible to find organic produce and soymilk in the supermarket. The timing is right to make that healthy change without having to look too far for the products.

The main goal of this cookbook is to help you make the transition to a more nutritious, yet elegant, way of cooking with simple, easy-to-prepare techniques! For those of you who have experienced the art of vegetarian cooking, you may also find that the recipes provided will give you new avenues to explore in this exciting cuisine.

For your convenience we have included a "shopping smart list" that can assist you in locating most of the items needed to produce the recipes in this book. The brand names listed will allow you to request these items from your local natural foods store.

In order to assist you with a well-rounded menu plan, there are 4 weeks of sample dinner menus and a basic lunch menu located in the back of the book. Feel free to interchange other favorites into your meal plans. The sample menus are similar to our weekly programs at the spa. For those of you who have visited the spa, there should be a sense of comfort knowing you have already experienced the success of these dishes.

Making vegetarian foods tasty and interesting for children who are not used to eating them is sometimes a challenge. In the index there is an asterisk beside recipes that kids have particularly enjoyed.

I certainly hope that my passion for food and pleasure can help you attain that level of good health and happiness we all wish to have.

Food Combining Made Simple

When you first visit The Regency House Health Spa, you may experience an initial shock. We recommend some rules of eating and food combining that will restructure your eating habits. The beauty of this situation is that with this shock comes a newfound knowledge of how we should be treating our bodies in the first place!

It will not take very long to understand the few basic concepts of our cuisine. After that you will find yourself becoming more self aware of the proper time for adequate digestion and be able to make more nutritious choices when planning your meals.

For your convenience and peace of mind when making decisions at meal time, we have listed below the simple rules to follow :

1. Avoid the drinking of any beverages, including water, 15 to 30 minutes before and after eating to allow for proper digestion.

2. When eating any melons, do not combine with any other fruit or vegetable. Melons digest very quickly, usually in about 30 minutes. We do not want to interfere with this digestive process. Melons include cantaloupe, honeydew, watermelon, casaba, and Crenshaw.

3. The same holds true for eating other fruits. Eat fruit alone. Do not eat any member of the melon group at that time.

4. Vegetables and leafy greens like Romaine lettuce, celery, and cucumbers combine quite well with fruit and will help modify any unstable reactions you may have to the sugar content of the fruit.

5. Eat proteins and starches separately, and combine them with salads and vegetables. This rule becomes more important if you are eating animal protein. If for example you eat a piece of fish, do not eat it with rice or potatoes. Eat it with salad and cooked vegetables. Animal proteins will increase the sugar index of any carbohydrates you eat them with and will make it harder for you to lose weight.

6. We do not recommend regular or decaffeinated coffee of any kind. They drain the body of its minerals and are usually heavily sprayed with pesticides. There are wonderful coffee substitutes available made from roasted chicory leaves that will provide you with the aroma without the effects of caffeine. Consult our Shopping Smart List on pages 10 and 11 for brand name natural foods.

THE VEGETARIAN PYRAMID

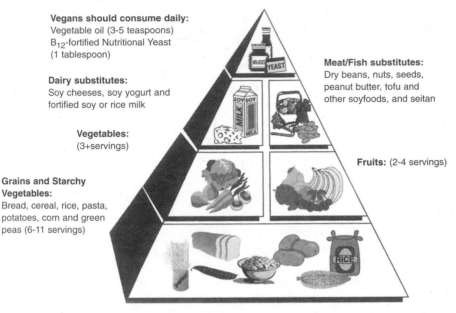

Vegans should consume daily:
Vegetable oil (3-5 teaspoons)
B_{12}-fortified Nutritional Yeast
(1 tablespoon)

Dairy substitutes:
Soy cheeses, soy yogurt and
fortified soy or rice milk

Vegetables:
(3+servings)

**Grains and Starchy
Vegetables:**
Bread, cereal, rice, pasta,
potatoes, corn and green
peas (6-11 servings)

Meat/Fish substitutes:
Dry beans, nuts, seeds,
peanut butter, tofu and
other soyfoods, and seitan

Fruits: (2-4 servings)

Good Health: The vegetarian pyramid recommends 3 or more servings a day of vegetables with a serving equal to ½ cup cooked or chopped raw vegetables or 1 cup raw leafy vegetables.

Vegetarian Food Pyramid: What's a Serving?

Grains and Starchy Vegetables
***6 to 11 servings a day:**
1 slice bread (choose calcium-
fortified bread if you don't
consume dairy products)
½ roll or bagel
1 tortilla
1 ounce ready-to-eat cereal
(vegans choose B_{12}-fortified
cereal) or ½ cup cooked
cereal rice or pasta
3 to 4 crackers
3 cups popcorn
½ cup corn
1 medium potato
½ cup green peas

Vegetables
***3 or more servings a day:**
½ cup cooked or chopped raw
vegetables
1 cup raw leafy vegetables
¾ cup vegetable juice

Meat/Fish Substitutes
***2-3 servings a day:**
1 cup cooked dry beans, peas,
or lentils
½ cup shelled nuts
¾ tablespoon peanut butter
¾ tablespoon tahini
⅓ to ½ cup seeds
8 ounces bean curd or tofu (a
source of calcium for those
who don't consume dairy
products)

Dairy substitutes
***2 servings per day for adults,
3 for preteens, 4 for teens:**
1 cup soy or rice milk with
calcium and vitamin D if
you don't consume dairy
products
1½ ounces soy cheese

Fruits
***2 to 4 servings a day:**
1 medium hand-held piece of
fruit
½ cup canned, chopped or
cooked fruit
¾ cup fruit juice

Plus for Vegans
3 to 5 teaspoons vegetable oil (for
calories and essential fatty acid);
vegans who don't include the
fortified products suggested in the
other food groups could benefit from
1 tablespoon blackstrap molasses
(for iron and calcium) and should
consume either 1 tablespoon
nutritional yeast fortified with B_{12} or
a vitamin supplement containing
B_{12}.

A Guide to "Shopping Smart"

For your convenience we have included a "healthy shopping list" to assist you in shopping smart at natural foods stores as well as your local supermarket.

There are many enriched products in the marketplace today ranging from breads to pastas. The name brands on our list are not enriched or refined products. At the very least, these products taste as good as any of the foods we have come to know and love. Products unenriched with vitamins such as riboflavin, niacin, or thiamine tend to contain more of their natural germ and fiber-rich bran. These nutrients make foods more nutritionally sound and easier to digest.

Fruits and vegetables are at the core of a vegetarian lifestyle. We do suggest that you purchase organic products whenever possible. Knowing that your family's food has not been exposed to pesticides will give you much peace of mind. If you cannot obtain organic produce, it becomes even more important to wash fruits and vegetables before using them.

Washing Procedure

Method 1. Fill your sink with cold water, 4 tablespoons of sea salt, and the juice of one lemon. Soak the fruits and vegetables for 5 to 10 minutes, then rinse in cool water and drain before using.

Method 2. Use 1 teaspoon of chlorine bleach to 1 gallon of cool water. Soak produce for 5 to 10 minutes, drain, and soak in fresh water another 5 to 10 minutes. If there is a bleach odor, rinse again and allow the produce to air out before consuming.

Method 3. To remove waxes, dip fruit in boiling water for 5 seconds. You may want to use tongs or grippers for safety.

Now that we are better equipped to "shop smart," the Vegetarian Magic in all of us will be alive and thrive!

SHOPPING SMART PRODUCT LIST

Dairy-free Products	Brand
Rice milk	Imagine Foods Rice Dream or Rice Milk by Westbrae
Soymilk	Westsoy Plus-Soy Milk, Imagine
Almond milk	Wholesome & Hearty Foods Almond Milk
Soy beverage	White Wave Silk Soy Beverage
Soy cheeses	Soya Kaas or White Wave
Soy Parmesan cheese	Soyco Light 'n Less or Soymage
Soy cream cheeses	Soya Kaas or White Wave
Soy yogurt	White Wave Dairyless Yogurt
Nonhydrogenated margarine	Spectrum Natural Spread, Earth Balance
Regular tofu	Nasoya or White Wave
Silken Tofu	Mori Nu Silken or Lite Silken
Tempeh	Light Life or White Wave
Egg-free mayonnaise	Nayonaise, Veganaise
Flavored tofu	White Wave

Condiments	Brand
Stone-ground mustards	Westbrae Natural Foods or Hain
Barley malt syrup	Eden Foods
Coffee	Natural Touch Roma Coffee Substitute, Teecino
Natural soy sauce or tamari	SanJ
Non-fermented soy sauce substitute	Bragg Liquid Aminos
Herbal teas	Celestial Seasonings, Yogi or Traditional Medicinals
Sweetener & fat replacer	Fruit Source
Sweeteners	Sucanat
Brown rice syrup	Westbrae Natural Foods, Lundberg

Organic Grains, Cereals & Pastas	Brand
Millet	Arrowhead Mills or Tree of Life
Legumes, beans	Arrowhead Mills or Tree of Life
Brown basmati rice	Arrowhead Mills, Lundberg, or Tree of Life
Rolled oats	Arrowhead Mills or Tree of Life
Pastas	DeBoles, Health Valley
Lupin pasta	IN-AG
Soba noodles	Eden Foods or other
Quinoa (Keen-wa)	Ancient Harvest
Whole wheat couscous	Casbah or Fantastic Foods

Prepared Foods	Brand
Egg replacer for baking	Ener-G Foods Inc.
Organic tomato	Muir Glen products
Pasta sauces	Ci'Bella by Westbrae, Muir Glenn
Vegetarian chilis	Hain or Health Valley
Mexican salsa	Tree of Life
Salad dressings	Blanchard & Blanchard or Ayla's Organics
Tahini	Joyva

Frozen	Brand
Vegan burgers	Wholesome and Hearty Foods
Vegetarian burgers and crumbles	Boca Burgers or Morningstar
Organic frozen pizzas	Soya Kaas, Amy's
Frozen meat substitutes	Gimme Lean or Morningstar
Frozen entrees	Amy's, Cedar Lane or Morningstar

COOKING TIPS

Cooking Without Oil

As you will notice, there are quite a few recipes in this book that use vegetable broth instead of oil to cook the vegtables. There is a good reason for this. The heating of oil (even if you use nutritious olive oil) leads to hydrogenation, where the molecular structure of the oil is rearranged in such a way that it can actually have a negative long-term effect on your cardiovascular health. Hydrogenation increases the amount of trans fatty acids in the oil, and these substances have been known to increase the LDL or "unhealthy cholesterol" that increases risk for heart disease. That is why most solidified vegetable fats, such as margarine and shortening (which require hydrogenation to be solid at room temperature), are no longer seen as a suitable replacement for animal fats.

As a rule of thumb, if I just want to soften or steam vegetables for a recipe, I use vegetable broth or yellow miso broth (1 tablespoon to a cup of liquid). Even when making marinara sauce, you can skip cooking the vegetables in olive oil; just put all the ingredients in a pot to simmer for hours or roast. You cannot tell the difference. You'll also avoid the unnecesary added calories you would have gotten from using oil.

We also "oven fry" dishes like our breaded eggplant Parmesan with hardly any oil and get the same delicious results that we would have if we had used more oil in our pans. I brush over the olive oil as I would pesto sauce. Similarly, if we're making a stir fry, I'll add a little roasted sesame oil to the dish after cooking. The flavor of this oil is so rich, a little will go a long way, and adding it at the end helps keep it from breaking down from the heat.

Cooking Beans

Soaking the beans for an hour or more will aid in reducing some of their gaseous effects. Also, beans cook faster, are digested more quickly, and taste even better when a small piece of kombu is added. Kombu is a sea vegetable that is high in B vitamins and iron. It is good for high blood pressure, cleanses the colon, aids the kidneys, and helps to prevent anemia. Kombu can be found in Oriental or natural foods stores and comes in either stiff, broad strands or in convenient-to-use flakes.

Jalapeño Pepper Alert (or any other hot pepper for that matter)

If you are a hot pepper afficionado, you probably don't need to read this note—but better safe than sorry. To avoid accidentally burning your body, wear rubber gloves. After processing the peppers and cleaning the knife and cutting board, wash the gloves and carefully remove them. Wash your hands well. While you are chopping the hot peppers and immediately after, do not touch your eyes, ears, or genitals no matter how badly they may itch. It is better to itch than to burn—trust me. (Caution: You will discover more body itches when chopping hot peppers than when doing any other activity in life short of an MRI.)

Anyway, enough of the visuals. Let's get back to cooking.

If you do not have gloves, be sure to place the peppers in with your other recipe ingredients immediately. Wash your knife, cutting board, and hands, especially your figure tips. In fact, wash your hands 2 or 3 more times before moving on. You will not regret it. If you don't have gloves, you can use baggies to cover your hands.

To get that perfect pepper flavor without the extreme heat, split the pepper down the middle and scoop out and discard the seeds. If you like your food really hot, by all means include the seeds. They are an extra source of heat. Julienne the pepper while holding onto the stem, then discard the stem. Finely chop the peppers while squinting. That way if the peppers splash you in the face, there is less of a chance the juice will go into your eyes. If you wear glasses, you don't need to squint.

Sodium-free Spice

This is an excellent condiment for steamed vegetables and soups.

2 tablespoons onion powder

2 tablespoons dried dill weed

2 tablespoons toasted sesame seeds

1 tablespoon finely chopped dried oregano

1 teaspoon celery seeds

1 teaspoon garlic powder

⅛ teaspoon cayenne pepper

Blend together and store in a spice jar.

APPETIZERS

BLACK BEAN AND CORN RELISH

Yield: 4 to 6 servings

This is a wonderfully refreshing salad for a cookout or as an accompaniment to a Mexican entree. If there is much leftover salad, try adding it to cooked brown rice for a Southwestern–style dish.

2 cups cooked black beans, drained and seasoned to taste

1½ cups cooked frozen corn

1 red bell pepper, chopped

1 small red onion, diced

2 vine-ripe tomatoes, diced

1 tablespoon minced garlic

1 tablespoon finely chopped cilantro

1 small jalapeño pepper, very finely chopped (for handling of hot peppers, see page 12)

½ teaspoon sea salt (optional)

1 Combine all the ingredients in a non-metallic bowl.

2 Adjust the seasonings to taste, and chill before serving.

Per serving: Calories 154, Protein 7 g, Fat 0 g, Carbohydrate 30 g, Fiber 7 g, Calcium 31 mg, Sodium 33 mg

BLACK BEAN HUMMUS

Yield: 8 to 10 servings

By not using tahini, this is a very flavorful, low-fat alternative to traditional hummus. Serve with raw vegetables, pita bread, and your favorite salad items or with nacho chips and Mexican salsa.

1 pound black beans

1 yellow onion

1 red bell pepper

2 quarts distilled or pure water

2 tablespoons minced garlic

2 teaspoons ground cumin

¼ teaspoon cayenne pepper

2 bay leaves

1 tablespoon finely chopped fresh cilantro

2 tablespoons Bragg Liquid Aminos

Per serving: Calories 97, Protein 6 g, Fat 0 g, Carbohydrate 18 g, Fiber 4 g, Calcium 25 mg, Sodium 96 mg

1 Soak the black beans in enough scalding water to cover for 1 to 2 hours. Drain in a colander. Chop the onion and bell pepper.

2 Bring the 2 quarts water to a boil, and add the soaked beans and remaining ingredients, except the cilantro and Bragg Liquid Aminos.

3 Simmer 1½ hours or until the beans are tender.

4 Remove from the stove and cool slightly.

5 Place the beans in a food processor or blender, and add enough of the cooking liquid to purée into a smooth paste.

6 Remove and place in a bowl. Fold in the cilantro and Bragg, adjust the seasonings to taste, and refrigerate until cool.

Chick-pea Hummus

Yield: 1 quart

This Middle Eastern appetizer dip can be served with pita bread and a salad. For a different flavor and color, add ⅔ cup roasted red peppers to this recipe. Process the peppers with the other ingredients

3 cups cooked, strained chick-peas, with liquid reserved

½ cup tahini

½ cup freshly squeezed lemon juice

1 tablespoon finely chopped Italian parsley

1 tablespoon Bragg Liquid Aminos

2 teaspoons minced garlic

½ teaspoon ground cumin

Dash of cayenne pepper

1 Process all the ingredients in a food processor or blender with enough of the reserved juice from the chick-peas to make a thick dip.

2 Adjust the seasonings to taste, and refrigerate.

Per ¼ cup: Calories 96, Protein 4 g, Fat 4 g, Carbohydrate 11 g, Fiber 2 g, Calcium 47 mg, Sodium 49 mg

EGGPLANT CAVIAR

Yield: 4 to 6 servings

This roasted eggplant, garlic, and sun–dried tomato dish is a great addition to a salad. It also serves well as a tasty, low–fat appetizer dip for crudités or pita crisps with imported olives

2 eggplants (about 2 pounds)

1 tablespoon extra-virgin olive oil

6 large cloves garlic, peeled

½ cup finely chopped sun-dried tomatoes, soaked and drained

3 tablespoons tomato purée

1 tablespoon balsamic vinegar

Dash of cayenne pepper

1 tablespoon Bragg Liquid Aminos

1 tablespoon finely chopped Italian parsley

Per serving: Calories 97, Protein 2 g, Fat 2 g, Carbohydrate 16 g, Fiber 4 g, Calcium 20 mg, Sodium 149 mg

1 Preheat the oven to 450°F. Cut the eggplant in half lengthwise, brush the cut side with some of the olive oil, and place on a baking sheet cut side down

2 Place the garlic cloves in the same pan, and also brush with the olive oil.

3 Bake for 40 to 45 minutes or until the eggplant is tender and the garlic is browned. Remove the garlic cloves before they blacken.

4 Let the eggplant cool and drain in a colander. When cool, scoop out the pulp with a spoon.

5 Place all the ingredients in a blender or food processor, and blend together.

6 Adjust the spices to taste, and refrigerate until very cold.

EGGPLANT NAPOLEON

Yield: 3 to 4 servings

*This cold appetizer has a beautiful vertical presentation and a taste to match its
appearance. We have also tried adding a grilled portobello mushroom cap in this recipe.
If you would like, serve it as a hot entree. Bake the assembled napoleon in a casserole lined
with marinara sauce at 400°F for 12 to 15 minutes. Serve it hot on a bed of quinoa pilaf.*

2 tablespoons extra-virgin olive oil

1 tablespoon chopped fresh basil

1 teaspoon minced garlic

1 teaspoon Bragg Liquid Aminos

1 medium eggplant, stem removed,
cut into ½-inch-thick rounds
(2 slices per person)

1 red bell pepper, cut into quarters,
stem and seeds removed

1 red onion, peeled, cored, and cut
into ¼-inch-thick slices

1½ cups balsamic vinegar

1 large vine-ripe tomato

1 yellow tomato

4 ounces soy mozzarella, cut into
⅛-inch slices (1 per person)

Per serving: Calories 231, Protein 10 g,
Fat 11 g, Carbohydrate 22 g, Fiber 6 g,
Calcium 259 mg, Sodium 343 mg

1 Preheat the oven on broil to
550°F.

2 To make a marinade, purée the
olive oil, basil, garlic, and Bragg
in a blender.

3 Place the sliced eggplant on a
lightly oiled sheet pan, and
brush with the marinade. Place
the pan on the top oven rack,
and broil for about 12 minutes,
or until the eggplant is a medium
brown. Only grill it on one side.
Remove and refrigerate until well
chilled.

4 Place the red pepper pieces skin
side up on an oiled sheet pan,
and roast on the top oven rack
for about 15 minutes or until the
skins are charred.

5 Remove the peppers from oven, place them in a plastic bag, and refrigerate until cool. Remove them from the bag, and the skins should come off easily. Slice the peppers into strips about ½ inch thick, and set aside.

6 While the eggplant and peppers are roasting, place the sliced red onion and balsamic vinegar in a saucepan, cover, and boil on a medium heat for about 30 minutes, or until the onions are tender. Remove from the heat and refrigerate uncovered until cool. When chilled, pour the onions into a strainer, and set aside for assembly. Save the reserved liquid to use as the dressing

7 Slice the tomatoes into ½-inch-thick slices.

8 To assemble, use a flat salad plate and spread out a handful of your favorite baby greens. Place 1 piece of the chilled roasted eggplant with the cooked side up on the center of the greens. On top of the eggplant, place 1 slice of red tomato, followed by 1 slice of the soy cheese and 1 slice of yellow tomato or, if unavailable, another red tomato slice. Place another piece of eggplant on top of the tomato. Sprinkle some of the sliced onion over the vegetable arrangement and around the sides. Drizzle some of the balsamic marinade over the eggplant stack, and garnish with the roasted pepper slices and a sprig of basil. Serve well chilled.

Guacamole Dip

Yield: approximately 2½ cups

There is not a faster, more delicious way to prepare this California favorite. We have found that Haas avocados, fully ripened, make the best–tasting dip.

3 ripe Haas avocados, scooped from their shells

2 tablespoons fresh lemon juice (about 1 lemon)

⅔ cup Mexican Salsa, page 62, or your favorite brand

¼ teaspoon sea salt (optional)

Per 2 tablespoons: Calories 54, Protein 1 g, Fat 4 g, Carbohydrate 4 g, Fiber 2 g, Calcium 5 mg, Sodium 81 mg

1 In a non-metallic bowl, mash the avocados and lemon juice together.

2 Fold in the salsa and adjust the seasonings to taste.

3 Return the pits of the avocado to the dip to maintain the color of the avocado.

4 For an even faster, creamier guacamole, place all the ingredients in a blender, and purée.

Vegetarian Chopped Chicken Liver

Yield: approximately 2½ cups

For those of us who remember that delicious, but rather calorie–laden holiday and year–round favorite, here is a nutritious alternative.

1 cup green beans, cut into 1-inch strips

1 teaspoon canola oil

1 yellow onion, thinly sliced

2 teaspoons minced garlic

8 ounces mushrooms, rinsed and cut in half

⅔ cup walnut pieces

1 tablespoon Bragg Liquid Aminos

Per 2 tablespoons: Calories 34, Protein 1 g, Fat 2 g, Carbohydrate 2 g, Fiber 1 g, Calcium 8 mg, Sodium 35 mg

1 Steam the green beans for 12 to 15 minutes until very tender, then refrigerate until cool.

2 Heat the canola oil in a large frying pan until very hot. Add the onions and sauté until golden brown. Add the garlic and continue to cook another minute or so.

3 Add the mushrooms and cook about 5 minutes until they have darkened in color. Remove from the heat and refrigerate until they have chilled.

4 Purée all the ingredients in a food processor or in batches in a blender until creamy. Adjust the seasonings to taste, and serve with rye bread or your favorite crackers.

Vine-Ripe Tomatoes and Soy Mozzarella with Pesto

Yield: up to 4 servings

This is one of the most popular appetizers at the spa. It can also be served as an entree.

1 head romaine lettuce

3 large vine-ripe tomatoes, sliced ½ inch thick

1 red or Vidalia onion, thinly sliced

4 ounces soy mozzarella, thinly sliced

⅓ cup Pesto Sauce, page 64

Per serving: Calories 187, Protein 9 g, Fat 11 g, Carbohydrate 10 g, Fiber 3 g, Calcium 232 mg, Sodium 281 mg

1 Core the romaine and rinse the leaves. Drain in the refrigerator.

2 Line a flat salad plate with the crispy romaine leaves.

3 Arrange 3 slices of tomato and 3 slices of onion alternately over the lettuce.

4 Arrange 2 slices of soy mozzarella over the tomatoes and onions.

5 With a tablespoon, drizzle a spoonful or two of the pesto sauce over the salad, and serve.

Salads

Angel Hair Pasta Pomodori Salad

Yield: 4 servings

This incredible salad is also excellent served hot.

3 quarts distilled or pure water

One 12-ounce box whole wheat or durum semolina angel hair pasta

3 vine-ripe tomatoes, coarsely chopped

1 tablespoon minced garlic

1 tablespoon red wine or balsamic vinegar

1 tablespoon finely chopped fresh basil

2 teaspoons brown rice syrup

Dash of cayenne pepper, or ⅛ teaspoon black pepper

¼ teaspoon sea salt, optional

1 tablespoon extra-virgin olive oil

⅔ cup soy or rice Parmesan

1 sprig basil for garnish

Per serving: Calories 263, Protein 13 g, Fat 7 g, Carbohydrate 39 g, Fiber 2 g, Calcium 16 mg, Sodium 372 mg

1 Bring the water to a gentle boil, and cook the pasta 4 to 6 minutes until al dente (tender but not soft).

2 Remove and strain in a colander, rinse with cool running water, and set aside.

3 Combine the remaining ingredients, except the soy Parmesan, in a mixing bowl.

4 In a large mixing bowl, place the drained pasta and add the tomato mixture.

5 Fold in ¾ of the soy Parmesan, and chill.

6 Serve cold and garnish with a basil sprig and the remaining soy Parmesan.

Asparagus and Shiitake Mushroom Salad

Yield: 4 servings

If you are tired of basic tossed salads, this one will surely liven up your first course.

1 pound fresh asparagus

4 ounces shiitake mushrooms

1 small red onion

4 plum tomatoes

3 stalks bok choy

⅔ cup Oriental Vinaigrette, page 49

2 tablespoons sesame seeds

Per serving: Calories 158, Protein 5 g, Fat 3 g, Carbohydrate 25 g, Fiber 6 g, Calcium 177 mg, Sodium 373 mg

1 Trim the white ends off the stalks of the asparagus, and cut the asparagus into 1½-inch pieces. Remove the stems from the shiitakes, and cut the caps in half. Thinly slice the red onion. Slice the tops from the plum tomatoes, and cut the tomatoes in quarters. Trim away the greens from the bok choy, and diagonally slice the stalks ½ inch thick.

2 Combine the asparagus, bok choy, and mushrooms, and lightly steam in a little water or vegetable broth for about 3 minutes, or until the asparagus is al dente. Drain the vegetables and refrigerate until chilled.

3 While the vegetables are cooling, prepare the vinaigrette dressing

4 Toss the dressing with the vegetables, refrigerate until chilled, and serve over fresh greens.

Avocado and Tomato Salad
with Lemon Dressing

Yield: 3 to 4 servings

Avocados are high in calories, but they are also very nutritious. They have been known to assist in the healing of ulcers. Eating tomatoes can also reduce the risk of prostate illness.

Lemon Dressing

½ cup fresh lemon juice

¼ cup distilled or pure water

¼ cup extra-virgin olive oil

1 tablespoon chopped fresh cilantro, basil, or oregano

¼ teaspoon sea salt

Dash of cayenne pepper

2 vine-ripe tomatoes, or 1 pint cherry tomatoes

1 red or Vidalia onion

2 ripe avocados

⅓ cup ripe black olives (Try different varieties of imported olives.)

Per serving: Calories 391, Protein 3 g, Fat 30 g, Carbohydrate 23 g, Fiber 6 g, Calcium 52 mg, Sodium 263 mg

1 Place all the dressing ingredients in a blender, and purée. Adjust the seasonings to taste.

2 Cut the whole tomatoes into wedges or the cherry tomatoes in half.

3 Cut the onion into ¼-inch slices.

4 Cut the avocados in half, remove the seeds, and scoop out with a spoon. Cut into ¾-inch slices, and place in a bowl with the remaining vegetables.

5 Toss the dressing with the vegetables, refrigerate until chilled, and serve over fresh greens.

Basmati Rice and Butternut Squash Salad

Yield: 6 to 8 servings

This salad can also be served hot as an entree or as a filling for stuff peppers or squash.

1 butternut squash

½ cup shelled pumpkin seeds

1 quart pure or distilled water

2 cups brown basmati rice or wild rice blend

3 scallions or chives, thinly sliced

2 tablespoons finely chopped fresh cilantro or basil

⅓ cup extra-virgin olive oil

1 tablespoon minced garlic

Dash of cayenne pepper

½ cup toasted unsalted soynuts, whole or halves

Per serving: Calories 352, Protein 10 g, Fat 17 g, Carbohydrate 40 g, Fiber 4 g, Calcium 66 mg, Sodium 6 mg

1 Cut the squash in half lengthwise, scoop out the seeds with a spoon, peel, and cut into ½ inch cubes. Lightly toast the pumpkin seeds in a 400°F oven for 10 minutes.

2 Bring the water to a boil, sprinkle in the rice, cover, and simmer for 25 minutes or until all water has evaporated and the rice is tender. Be careful not to overcook the rice, or it will split and become starchy.

3 While the rice is cooking, steam or cook the squash for about 10 to 12 minutes until tender, but not mushy. Place in the refrigerator to cool.

4 Spread the cooked rice on a cookie sheet, and refrigerate until cool. (If you are in a hurry, like I usually am, place the rice and squash in the freezer and stir often to cool quickly.)

5 Place the olive oil, garlic, and pepper in a blender, and process until smooth.

6 Place all the ingredients, except the soynuts, in a large bowl, and toss until thoroughly mixed. Adjust the seasonings to taste, and serve cold or hot with the soynuts as a garnish.

Bowtie Pasta Salad
with Sundried Tomatoes

Yield: 3 to 4 servings

This dish was initially created with grilled shrimp, chicken breast slices, or Cajun scallops. It was very easy to adapt to vegan cooking simply by removing the animal products. I am sure you have favorite recipes that can still be enjoyed in much the same way. Either serve cold or heat and serve hot as an entree. Garnish with basil sprigs. Try tricolored pasta for a more colorful dish.

2 quarts distilled or pure water

12 ounces bowtie pasta (farfalle)

⅔ cup sun-dried tomatoes

¼ cup extra-virgin olive oil

1 tablespoon balsamic vinegar

1 tablespoon chopped fresh basil leaves

2 teaspoons minced garlic

¼ teaspoon sea salt, optional

Dash of cayenne pepper, or ⅛ teaspoon black pepper

2 vine-ripe tomatoes, cut into wedges

Per serving: Calories 281, Protein 5 g, Fat 14 g, Carbohydrate 30 g, Fiber 2 g, Calcium 13 mg, Sodium 166 mg

1 Bring the water to a boil, add the pasta, and cook for 6 to 8 minutes until just tender, stirring occasionally. Strain in a colander, rinse with cool water, and strain again.

2 Soften the sun-dried tomatoes in hot water, and slice into julienne strips.

3 In a blender, purée the olive oil, vinegar, and spices.

4 In a large bowl, toss together the pasta, tomatoes, and blended oil. Adjust the seasonings to taste.

CAESAR SALAD

Yield: 6 to 8 servings

I am most proud of this low–fat, low–sodium version of classic Caesar salad. The balsamic vinegar gives it color and character, and the tofu gives it creaminess. The dressing will keep 5 to 7 days in the refrigerator.

2 heads romaine lettuce, cored
(Remove any brown spots.)

2 tablespoons fresh lemon juice

2 teaspoons minced garlic

1 tablespoon stone-ground mustard

2 tablespoons balsamic vinegar

2 tablespoons distilled or pure water

4 ounces extra-firm silken tofu, cubed

2 cups Pita Croutons, page 96

½ cup soy or rice Parmesan

Per serving: Calories 128, Protein 7 g,
Fat 4 g, Carbohydrate 14 g, Fiber 2 g,
Calcium 44 mg, Sodium 363 mg

1 Clean the lettuce and allow to crisp in the refrigerator for 1 hour.

2 In a blender, add the lemon juice, garlic, mustard, vinegar, water, tofu and purée.

3 Cut the lettuce and toss with the desired amount of dressing. Garnish with the pita croutons and soy Parmesan.

CREAMY NEW POTATO SALAD

Yield: 8 servings

This delicious salad is made with an eggless mayonnaise. The key to a creamy potato salad is to add your dressing while the potatoes are still warm. For an added twist, sprinkle in some Cajun spice for a New Orleans–style salad.

2 pounds red potatoes, unpeeled

1 red onion, chopped, or 3 scallions, sliced

1 large carrot, peeled and shredded

2 stalks celery, split down the middle lengthwise and thinly sliced

1 yellow or red bell pepper, chopped

1 cup Nayonaise or Veganaise

2 tablespoons stone-ground mustard

1 teaspoon celery seeds

Dash of cayenne pepper

½ teaspoon sea salt (optional)

Per serving: Calories 188, Protein 2 g, Fat 7 g, Carbohydrate 28 g, Fiber 3 g, Calcium 20 mg, Sodium 324 mg

1 Cut the potatoes into 1-inch cubes. If they are small, you can just cut them into quarters.

2 Bring a large pot of water to a boil, add the potatoes, and cook for 15 to 20 minutes until the potatoes are tender. Pierce the potatoes with a paring knife to be sure they are done. Pour the cooked potatoes into a strainer to drain, and set aside.

3 While the potatoes are cooking, prepare all the vegetables.

4 Transfer the potatoes to a large mixing bowl, add all the ingredients, and mix well. Adjust the spices as desired; cover and refrigerate until well chilled.

CURRIED LENTIL SALAD

Yield: 4 servings

This hearty salad is high in protein and could also be reheated as an entree.

3 quarts distilled or pure water

1 pound green or red lentils

2 bay leaves

1 Vidalia or other yellow onion, chopped

1 carrot, finely diced or shredded

2 stalks celery, diced

2 teaspoons curry powder

⅓ cup fresh lemon juice (from about 3 lemons)

2 tablespoons chopped fresh parsley

2 tablespoons Bragg Liquid Aminos

2 teaspoons minced garlic

Dash of cayenne pepper

1 In a large pot, bring the water to a boil. In a strainer rinse the lentils, checking for stones.

2 Add the lentils and bay leaves to the pot. Cover and simmer for about 30 minutes, stirring occasionally, until the lentils are tender. Skim the foam off the cooking liquid while stirring. Remove from the heat.

3 Strain the lentils and mix with the remaining ingredients. Adjust the seasonings to taste, and chill.

Per serving: Calories 168, Protein 11 g, Fat 0 g, Carbohydrate 31 g, Fiber 4 g, Calcium 48 mg, Sodium 358 mg

Fat-free Cucumber-Dill Salad

Yield: 3 to 4 servings

This salad is especially colorful served on a bed of field greens or mesclun lettuce.

3 large cucumbers, peeled

1 red onion

½ cup apple cider vinegar

⅔ cup brown rice syrup

Dash of cayenne pepper

1 tablespoon chopped fresh dill

Per serving: Calories 244, Protein 1 g, Fat 0 g, Carbohydrate 58 g, Fiber 4 g, Calcium 53 mg, Sodium 9 mg

1   Cut the cucumbers and onion into ½-inch slices. Toss together in a large bowl, and set aside.

2   Make a marinade by processing the vinegar, rice syrup, and pepper in a blender.

3   Toss the vegetables with the dressing and dill, and refrigerate. Adjust the seasonings to taste. Stir occasionally to distribute the marinade evenly.

Clockwise from left: Caesar Salad, p. 29, Black Bean and Corn Relish, p. 14, and Eggplant Caviar, p. 17, surrounded by roasted peppers, artichoke hearts, hearts of palm, and mesclun greens.

GRANNY ANNIE'S WALDORF SALAD

This recipe is dedicated to Ann Rogers. This is her favorite holiday salad. I replaced the mayonnaise with a tastier, more nutritious yogurt dressing.

3 Red Delicious apples

3 Granny Smith apples, or a combination of apples and D'Anjou pears

⅓ cup lemon juice

3 celery stalks, diced

1 cup red or green seedless grapes

⅔ cup raisins

½ cup walnut pieces

Banana Yogurt Dressing:

½ cup vanilla soy yogurt

⅓ cup fresh orange juice

1 ripe banana

½ teaspoon cinnamon

1 teaspoon vanilla extract

1 Core and chop the apples (and pears, if using). Place in a large bowl, and toss with the lemon juice to prevent discoloring.

2 Place the dressing ingredients in a blender, and puree until creamy.

3 Add the remaining salad ingredients and the dressing with the apples, and serve well chilled.

Per serving: Calories 213, Protein 3 g, Fat 6 g, Carbohydrate 41 g, Fiber 6 g, Calcium 33 mg, Sodium 23 mg

Clockwise from left: Black and White Bean Soup, p. 81, Mexican Tortilla Soup, pp. 82–83, and Spring Vegetable Soup

GRILLED VEGETABLE SALAD

Yield: 4 to 6 servings

We created this salad as a means of using our leftover grilled vegetables from dinner. What we didn't know was how incredible it would be on its own!

3 portobello mushrooms

1 unpeeled eggplant

2 yellow squash

2 zucchini

2 roasted red bell peppers (See page 205.)

Marinade

¼ cup canola oil or olive oil

1 teaspoon minced garlic

2 teaspoons chopped fresh oregano, or 1 teaspoon dried

Dash of cayenne pepper

1 Remove the stems from the portobello mushrooms, and scrape off the gills on their undersides. Slice the remaining vegetables ½ inch thick on an angle, place in a large pan, and set aside.

2 Turn your grill to its highest setting for 5 minutes, or until very hot.

3 Place all the marinade ingredients in a blender, and process to emulsify the flavors.

4 Brush the marinade over the cut vegetables, and place brushed side down on the grill.

5 While the vegetables are grilling, brush the tops of them with more of the marinade.

Dressing

¼ cup extra-virgin olive oil

1 tablespoon Bragg Liquid Aminos

2 tablespoons distilled or pure water

2 tablespoons fresh lemon juice

1 tablespoon balsamic vinegar

1 tablespoon chopped fresh herbs (basil, oregano, or tarragon or any of your favorite fresh herbs—dry herbs will do in a pinch)

1 teaspoon minced garlic

Dash of cayenne pepper

Per serving: Calories 186, Protein 5 g, Fat 10 g, Carbohydrate 19 g, Fiber 6 g, Calcium 64 mg, Sodium 16 mg

6 When dark grill marks appear on the vegetables, flip over and grill on the other side. The mushrooms may need to cook longer than the other vegetables to become tender.

7 Place all the grilled vegetables in the refrigerator until cool.

8 Place all the dressing ingredients in a blender, and process, or whip rapidly by hand until well blended.

9 Remove the chilled vegetables from the refrigerator, and toss lightly with the dressing.

10 Refrigerate for 1 to 2 hours, and serve.

Greek Pasta Salad

Yield: 6 to 8 servings

This flavorful pasta can also be served as a hot entree.

3 quarts distilled or pure water

1 pound tri-colored rotini pasta

Dressing

2 tablespoons chopped fresh basil
leaves

1 tablespoon minced garlic

½ cup extra-virgin olive oil

¼ teaspoon sea salt, optional

Dash of cayenne pepper, or
⅛ teaspoon black pepper

3 ounces sun-dried tomatoes,
softened in scalded water and
coarsely cut

⅓ cup sliced black olives

⅓ cup sliced green olives with
pimientos

⅓ cup soy Parmesan

1 sprig basil, for garnish

1 Bring the water to a rolling boil,
add the pasta, and stir frequently. Cook for 6 to 8 minutes, or
until just tender.

2 Place the pasta in a colander,
and quickly rinse with cool
water.

3 Combine the basil, garlic, olive
oil, salt, and cayenne in a
blender to make a well-emulsi-
fied dressing.

4 In a large mixing bowl, toss the
pasta with the dressing and add
the remaining ingredients.

5 Refrigerate until cool and garnish
with the soy Parmesan and a
basil sprig.

Per serving: Calories 294, Protein 7 g,
Fat 19 g, Carbohydrate 27 g, Fiber 3 g,
Calcium 10 mg, Sodium 302 mg

Heart-to-Heart Salad
(Marinated Hearts of Palm and Artichokes)

Yield: 4 servings

Hearts of palm come from the cabbage palm tree. There is a festival every February in La Belle, Florida, honoring this vegetable. (The old timers call it "swamp cabbage.")

1 small red bell pepper

1 small yellow or orange bell pepper

One 12-ounce can hearts of palm, drained and sliced ½ inch thick on an angle

One 12-ounce can artichoke hearts, drained and cut in half

⅓ cup drained ripe black olives

⅓ cup drained green olives with pimientos

1 pint cherry tomatoes, cut in half, or 2 vine-ripe tomatoes, quartered (optional)

Per serving: Calories 233, Protein 3 g, Fat 15 g, Carbohydrate 18 g, Fiber 6 g, Calcium 55 mg, Sodium 321 mg

Marinade

¼ cup extra-virgin olive oil

¼ cup apple cider vinegar

2 tablespoons fresh lemon juice

1 teaspoon minced garlic

2 teaspoons oregano leaves

Dash of cayenne pepper, or ⅛ teaspoon black pepper

1 Cut the bell peppers into 1-inch cubes, and toss all the vegetables in a large bowl.

2 Place all the marinade ingredients in a blender, and purée for 30 seconds. Pour over the tossed vegetables, and combine well. Serve on a bed of greens.

Seaweed Cole Slaw

Yield: 6 to 8 servings

Wakame is prepared from a large brown seaweed, and like other seaweeds it contains more minerals than do land plants. This is a much more healthful and colorful version of traditional cole slaw. We serve it to complement our vegetable sushi rolls, page 150–52.

1 package (3 ounces) wakame

2 tablespoons sesame seeds

½ head green cabbage (about 6 cups)

3 stalks bok choy, with leaves trimmed, sliced ⅛-inch thick

1 large carrot, shredded

1 small daikon radish, peeled and shredded

1½ cups Oriental Vinaigrette, page 49

Per serving: Calories 113, Protein 3 g, Fat 2 g, Carbohydrate 20 g, Fiber 4 g, Calcium 131 mg, Sodium 467 mg

1 Soak the wakame in warm water for 15 minutes, then strain. With the tip of a knife, trim the wakame leaves away from the tough stem that runs along the center of most large leaves, and cut the leaves into thick strips.

2 Toast the sesame seeds by either baking at 400°F for 12 to 15 minutes or sautéing in a dry pan over medium-high heat until browned, stirring occasionally.

3 Core and slice or shred the cabbage ¼ inch thick or less. Toss all the vegetables in a large bowl with the vinaigrette and half the sesame seeds.

4 Refrigerate until well chilled. Garnish with the remaining sesame seeds. This salad should keep for up to 2 days in the refrigerator.

Soba Noodle Salad WITH ORIENTAL VEGETABLES

Soba noodles are made from buckwheat flour or a combination of buckwheat and whole wheat flour. They're prepared like regular pasta and are a valuable source of protein.

12 ounces soba noodles

2 carrots

4 scallions

½ pound snow peas, with stems removed

2 cups broccoli florettes

1 cup Oriental Vinaigrette, page 49

2 tablespoons toasted sesame seeds

Per serving: Calories 370, Protein 11 g, Fat 4 g, Carbohydrate 72 g, Fiber 5 g, Calcium 108 mg, Sodium 307 mg

1 Cook the soba noodles for about 8 to 10 minutes until just tender; rinse with cool water and chill.

2 Slice the carrots and scallions ¼ inch long on an angle and the snow peas 1 inch long on an angle. Cook or steam the carrots, snow peas, and broccoli until just tender, then chill.

3 In a large bowl, toss the soba noodles, vegetables, and vinaigrette.

4 Refrigerate until cool, tossing from time to time to incorporate the flavors. Garnish with toasted sesame seeds, and serve.

TABBOULEH

Yield: 4 servings

You may have seen this traditional Lebanese salad spelled or prepared differently. I enjoy the chick–peas for added texture and protein.

1 cup bulgur wheat

2 cups distilled or pure water

1 cup cooked chick-peas, drained

2 tablespoons chopped Italian parsley

1 tablespoon chopped peppermint leaves

1 tablespoon minced garlic

2 vine-ripe tomatoes, diced

⅓ cup fresh lemon juice

1 small red onion, diced

1 tablespoon Bragg Liquid Aminos

Dash of cayenne pepper

Per serving: Calories 201, Protein 8 g, Fat 1 g, Carbohydrate 39 g, Fiber 6 g, Calcium 41 mg, Sodium 177 mg

1 Bring the water to a boil, stir in the bulgur, turn off the heat, and cover for 15 minutes, stirring from time to time until the water is absorbed.

2 Place the cooked bulgur in a bowl, and chill while preparing the other vegetables.

3 Combine all the remaining ingredients with the bulgur, and adjust the seasonings to taste. Serve well chilled.

White Bean and Pesto Salad

Yield: 4 to 6 servings

This hearty salad is bursting with flavor and color.

1 pound navy beans or Great Northern beans

2½ quarts distilled or pure water

2 bay leaves

⅛ teaspoon cayenne pepper

1 cup Pesto Sauce, page 64

1 red bell pepper

1 bunch scallions

Per serving: Calories 329, Protein 9 g, Fat 22 g, Carbohydrate 21 g, Fiber 5 g, Calcium 72 mg, Sodium 99 mg

1 Soak the beans in enough scalding water to cover for 1 to 2 hours.

2 Bring the distilled water to a boil. Drain the beans and add to the boiling water with the bay leaves. Cook for 1 hour or until the beans are tender, but not mushy.

3 While the beans are cooking, prepare the pesto sauce and dice the bell pepper and scallions.

4 When the beans are tender, remove and drain in a colander.

5 Chill the beans, then fold in the pesto sauce and remaining ingredients. Marinate for ½ hour or more to maximize the flavors.

WILD RICE SALAD WITH RASPBERRY DRESSING

Yield: 4 servings

Overcook the rice until it splits so you'll have the texture you want for this salad.
Raisins are a nice option if cranberries are unavailable.

1 quart distilled or pure water

1 cup wild rice

1 cup Raspberry Vinaigrette Dressing,
    page 52

1 tablespoon poppy seeds (optional)

¼ cup toasted almond slices

⅓ cup sun-dried cranberries

⅓ cup sun-dried cherries

Per serving: Calories 292, Protein 5 g,
Fat 5 g, Carbohydrate 56 g, Fiber 5 g,
Calcium 54 mg, Sodium 149 mg

1 Bring the distilled water to a boil, and add the wild rice.

2 Cook the rice about 40 to 45 minutes until it is tender and splits. Strain the rice and cool in the refrigerator.

3 While the rice is cooling, prepare the dressing and toast the almonds.

4 When the rice is cool, add all the remaining ingredients and serve cold.

Salad
Dressings

Many of the salad dressings in this chapter are fat–free, others have been emulsified with tofu, tahini, or olive oil and have less than 1 gram of saturated fat per serving.

Apple-Mustard Dressing

Yield: 2½ cups

This dressing is so simple yet so full of flavor. For best quality, use within 5 days.

3 red or yellow apples
⅓ cup stone-ground mustard
⅓ cup brown rice syrup
¼ cup fresh lemon juice

1 Rinse, core, and cut the apples into wedges.

2 Combine all the ingredients in a blender, and purée thoroughly.

Per tablespoon: Calories 17, Protein 0 g, Fat 0 g, Carbohydrate 3 g, Fiber 0 g, Calcium 1 mg, Sodium 53 mg

Citrus-Poppy Seed Dressing

Yield: approximately 3 cups

This dressing goes especially well with a spinach or red leaf lettuce salad. It will keep well for up to 5 days in your refrigerator.

1 cup freshly squeezed orange juice
½ cup lime juice
¼ cup balsamic vinegar
1 tablespoon stone-ground mustard
½ cup brown rice syrup
Dash of cayenne pepper
8 ounces extra-firm silken tofu,
    drained and cut into cubes
1 tablespoon poppy seeds

1 Place all the ingredients in a blender, and purée.

Per tablespoon: Calories 18, Protein 0 g, Fat 0 g, Carbohydrate 4 g, Fiber 0 g, Calcium 5 mg, Sodium 11 mg

Balsamic Vinaigrette

Yield: 3½ cups

This is one of our most requested dressings. The older the balsamic vinegar, the richer the flavor will be. It should keep in the refrigerator for 5 to 7 days.

1 red apple

1 vine-ripe tomato

1 small red onion

1 small avocado (optional)

2 cups distilled or pure water

2 tablespoons chopped fresh basil

1 tablespoon chopped fresh oregano

1 teaspoon chopped fresh thyme

1 tablespoon minced fresh garlic

⅓ cup balsamic vinegar

¼ cup fresh lemon juice (about 2 lemons)

2 tablespoons stone-ground mustard

Dash of cayenne pepper

¼ cup extra-virgin olive oil (optional)

1 Core and quarter the apple and tomato. Peel and quarter the onion, and scoop the avocado from its shell.

2 Place all the ingredients in blender, and purée thoroughly.

3 Adjust the water to obtain the preferred consistency and the spices to taste.

Per tablespoon: Calories 4, Protein 0 g, Fat 0 g, Carbohydrate 1 g, Fiber 0 g, Calcium 1 mg, Sodium 15 mg

CREAMY FRENCH DRESSING

Yield: about 1½ cups

You'll have a hard time finding a more nutritious French dressing recipe than this one. For best quality, use within 5 days.

1 cup fresh carrot juice

¼ cup extra-virgin olive oil

3 tablespoons stone-ground mustard

2 tablespoons freshly squeezed lemon juice (about 1 lemon)

1 teaspoon minced fresh garlic

Dash of cayenne pepper

1 Combine all the ingredients in a blender, and purée thoroughly.

Per tablespoon: Calories 25, Protein 0 g, Fat 2 g, Carbohydrate 1 g, Fiber 0 g, Calcium 3 mg, Sodium 21 mg

CREAMY GARLIC DRESSING

Yield: approximately 2½ cups

This dressing has many uses. It can add flavor to baked potatoes, steamed vegetables, and salads. For best quality, use within 5 days.

1¼ cups rice milk or soymilk

One 12.3-ounce package firm silken tofu, drained and cubed

¼ cup fresh lemon or lime juice

1 tablespoon minced fresh garlic

1 tablespoon Bragg Liquid Aminos

2 tablespoons chopped fresh herbs, such as basil, tarragon, oregano, or dill (optional)

Dash of cayenne pepper, or ⅛ teaspoon black pepper

1 Combine all the ingredients in a blender, and purée thoroughly.

Per tablespoon: Calories 8, Protein 1 g, Fat 0 g, Carbohydrate 1 g, Fiber 0 g, Calcium 3 mg, Sodium 20 mg

FAT-FREE ITALIAN DRESSING

Yield: approximately 2 cups

The vegetables act as the emulsifier in this dressing, therefore no olive oil is needed. It will keep for up to 5 days in the refrigerator; blend well before reusing.

1 small red onion

1 large red bell pepper

1 large yellow or orange bell pepper

½ cup apple cider vinegar

⅓ cup brown rice syrup

1 tablespoon finely chopped fresh
   oregano

1 tablespoon minced garlic

Dash of cayenne pepper

½ cup distilled or pure water
   (optional)

1 Peel the onion, seed the bell peppers, and cut all of them into quarters.

2 Purée all the ingredients together in a blender at high speed for about 1 minute. Add water if a thinner dressing is desired.

Per tablespoon: Calories 13, Protein 0 g, Fat 0 g, Carbohydrate 4 g, Fiber 0 g, Calcium 1 mg, Sodium 0 mg

Mustard-Tahini Dressing

Yield: 1½ to 2 cups

This is hands down our guests' favorite dressing. It has such a tantalizing array of taste sensations. The dressing will keep well for up to 1 month in the refrigerator. It may need to be thinned with a little cool water upon reusing. I recommend using Joyva brand tahini.

½ to ⅔ cup water (enough to provide the desired consistency)

½ cup fresh lemon juice

½ cup tahini

⅓ cup brown rice syrup

3 tablespoons stone-ground mustard

1 tablespoon Bragg Liquid Aminos

2 teaspoons minced garlic

1 tablespoon chopped fresh parsley

Dash of cayenne pepper

1 Place all the ingredients in a blender, and process until smooth.

2 Add more water slowly if you prefer a thinner consistency.

Per tablespoon: Calories 40, Protein 1 g, Fat 2 g, Carbohydrate 4 g, Fiber 0 g, Calcium 19 mg, Sodium 72 mg

Orange Yogurt Dressing

Yield: 1¾ cups

This is a wonderfully refreshing sauce to go with your favorite tropical fruits. It can also be used as a replacement for mayonnaise in a Waldorf salad.

2 teaspoons orange zest (obtain from the oranges before cutting and squeezing)

½ cup fresh orange juice (about 4 oranges)

¾ cup vanilla soy yogurt

½ cup brown rice syrup

1 Combine all the ingredients in a mixing bowl with a wire whip until smooth.

Per tablespoon: Calories 27, Protein 0 g, Fat 0 g, Carbohydrate 6 g, Fiber 0 g, Calcium 1 mg, Sodium 2 mg

Oriental Vinaigrette

Yield: approximately 2½ cups

This dressing also serves as a marinade for Seaweed Cole Slaw, page 38, Chinese vegetable salads, or grilled tofu steaks. It should keep for 7 days or more in the refrigerator.

1 cup pure or distilled water

½ cup low-sodium tamari or shoyu

½ cup brown rice syrup

⅓ cup rice vinegar or cider vinegar

1 vine-ripe tomato, quartered

2 tablespoons toasted sesame seeds

1 tablespoon minced garlic

1 teaspoon vegetarian chili paste

1 teaspoon toasted sesame oil

1 Place all the ingredients in blender, and purée thoroughly.

2 Adjust the water and spices to satisfy your taste and achieve the right consistency.

Per tablespoon: Calories 20, Protein 0 g, Fat 0 g, Carbohydrate 4 g, Fiber 0 g, Calcium 6 mg, Sodium 121 mg

Peanut Butter Dressing

Yield: approximately 3 cups

*This dressing is so-o-o good you may find yourself drinking it as a beverage sometimes!
It is great over Oriental-style vegetables, salads, and pasta.*

1 cup pure or distilled water

⅔ cup sodium-free peanut butter

½ cup low-sodium tamari or soy
  sauce

½ cup brown rice syrup

⅓ cup rice vinegar

1 vine-ripe tomato, quartered
  (optional)

2 tablespoons toasted sesame seeds

1 tablespoon minced garlic

1 teaspoon vegetarian chili paste or
  other hot sauce

1 teaspoon toasted sesame oil

1 Place all the ingredients in a
  blender, and process until
  smooth.

2 Adjust the spices and peanut butter to taste, and the water to
  achieve the desired consistency.

Per tablespoon: Calories 34, Protein 1 g,
Fat 2 g, Carbohydrate 4 g, Fiber 0 g,
Calcium 6 mg, Sodium 100 mg

Pineapple-Mustard Dressing

Yield: 3 cups

This gives a special flavor to a spinach or leafy salad. For best quality, use within 5 days.

1 cup apple juice

1 cup freshly squeezed orange juice

1 cup fresh pineapple chunks

2 tablespoons stone-ground mustard

½ ripe avocado, scooped from the shell

1 teaspoon minced garlic

1 Combine all the ingredients in a blender, and purée thoroughly.

Per tablespoon: Calories 12, Protein 0 g, Fat 0 g, Carbohydrate 2 g, Fiber 0 g, Calcium 2 mg, Sodium 18 mg

Sweet and Spicy Mustard Dressing

Yield: 1½ cups

This dressing has a multitude of uses. It may be used as a marinade, dip, or dressing.

⅓ cup stone-ground mustard

¼ cup water

¼ cup brown rice vinegar

½ cup brown rice syrup

2 teaspoons minced ginger

1 tablespoon Sucanat

2 tablespoons low-sodium tamari

1 tablespoon toasted sesame oil

1 tablespoon hot sauce

1 teaspoon umeboshi plum vinegar (optional)

1 Place all ingredients in a blender, and process until creamy. Adjust the seasonings to taste.

Per tablespoon: Calories 34, Protein 0 g, Fat 1 g, Carbohydrate 0 g, Fiber 0 g, Calcium 1 mg, Sodium 171 mg

RASPBERRY-TAHINI DRESSING

Yield: approximately 1½ cups

My good friend and colleague Chef Ken Hubscher collaborated on this recipe. The dressing should keep for 5 to 7 days in the refrigerator. If it becomes too thick, add a little cool water upon reusing until the desired consistency is attained.

½ pint fresh raspberries, sorted and rinsed

¼ cup rice milk or soymilk

¼ cup brown rice syrup

3 tablespoons tahini

1 tablespoon tamari

2 tablespoons apple cider or raspberry vinegar

1 Place all the ingredients in a blender, and purée thoroughly. If the raspberries are too sour, add more brown rice syrup.

Per tablespoon: Calories 26, Protein 0 g, Fat 0 g, Carbohydrate 4 g, Fiber 0 g, Calcium 9 mg, Sodium 44 mg

RASPBERRY VINAIGRETTE

Yield: approximately 2 cups

Raspberries serve as a wonderful emulsifier for this fat-free dressing. It will keep for 5 to 7 days in the refrigerator.

½ cup apple cider vinegar

1 tablespoon chopped fresh basil

1 pint fresh raspberries, sorted and rinsed

½ cup brown rice syrup

1 Purée all the ingredients in a blender. If the raspberries are too sour, add more brown rice syrup to sweeten.

Per tablespoon: Calories 21, Protein 0 g, Fat 0 g, Carbohydrate 5 g, Fiber 0 g, Calcium 2 mg, Sodium 0 mg

Tarragon Vinaigrette

Yield: approximately 1½ cups

This dressing goes particularly well over a baby spinach salad with mushrooms, red onions, and pita croutons. It should keep for 5 to 7 days in the refrigerator.

⅓ cup apple cider vinegar

¼ cup pure or distilled water

4 ounces firm silken tofu

2 tablespoons stone-ground mustard

2 tablespoons brown rice syrup

2 tablespoons fresh lemon juice

1 teaspoon minced garlic

1 tablespoon chopped fresh tarragon, or 2 teaspoons dried

Per tablespoon: Calories 11, Protein 0 g, Fat 0 g, Carbohydrate 1 g, Fiber 0 g, Calcium 2 mg, Sodium 37 mg

1 Place all the ingredients, except the tarragon, in a blender, and purée thoroughly.

2 Add the tarragon to the blender, and pulse to incorporate.

3 Refrigerate the dressing until chilled. This will enhance its flavor.

Traditional Tahini Dressing

Yield: 3 cups

Adding basil to this recipe gives it a sweeter, more enjoyable flavor. This dressing will keep for up to 1 month in the refrigerator. It may need to be thinned with a little cool water upon reusing.

2 cups distilled or pure water

½ cup fresh lemon juice

⅓ cup barley malt or brown rice syrup

1 teaspoon ground cumin

1 tablespoon minced garlic

1 tablespoon chopped fresh basil (optional)

1 cup tahini

1 In a blender, combine all the ingredients except the tahini.

2 Add the tahini slowly until you reach the desired consistency.

CAUTION: Do not place the tahini in the blender until last. It is very heavy and has been known to burn up a blender motor before its time!

Per tablespoon: Calories 36, Protein 1 g, Fat 2 g, Carbohydrate 4 g, Fiber 0 g, Calcium 21 mg, Sodium 4 mg

Sauces

The sauces in this book are free of butter, margarine, and flour. They have been emulsi-fied at times with silken tofu. All the sauces contain less than 1 gram of saturated fat per serving.

ALFREDO SAUCE

Yield: 1 quart

This sauce is very similar to the original Alfredo sauce in flavor and texture, however it is cholesterol–free and lower in fat. It can be used with your favorite pastas or you can interchange other fat–free soy cheeses in place of the soy Parmesan to create an au gratin sauce.

2 cups soymilk or rice milk

One 12.3-ounce box low-fat extra-firm or firm silken tofu

1 teaspoon minced garlic

Dash of ground nutmeg

Dash of cayenne pepper, or ¼ teaspoon ground black pepper

1 teaspoon yellow miso

1 cup soy or rice Parmesan

2 teaspoons chopped fresh basil or parsley (optional)

1 Place all the ingredients, except the miso, soy Parmesan and basil or parsley, in a blender, and purée.

2 Place the blended mixture in a saucepan, and simmer until hot, stirring occasionally.

3 Whip in the miso, soy Parmesan and basil or parsley, and adjust the seasonings as desired. Serve hot. Be careful not to boil the sauce as it may separate.

Per ¼ cup: Calories 45, Protein 5 g, Fat 2 g, Carbohydrate 2 g, Fiber 1 g, Calcium 7 mg, Sodium 160 mg

CHILI CON QUESO

Yield: approximately 2½ cups

This versatile, fat–free sauce is good as a dip for tortilla chips or as a spicy cheese topping for a broccoli or cauliflower casserole.

1 large vine-ripe tomato, chopped

4 scallions, cut into ¼-inch slices

1 small red bell pepper, diced

1 jalapeño pepper, finely chopped (for note on handling hot peppers, see page 12)

1 tablespoon finely chopped cilantro

8 ounces soy cheddar, shredded

1 teaspoon hot sauce (optional)

1 In a saucepan, combine the tomato, scallions, peppers, and cilantro, and simmer until the vegetables are tender.

2 Stir in the soy cheddar until it is fully melted. Adjust the seasonings to taste.

3 Lower the heat to warm, and cover until served.

Per ¼ cup: Calories 67, Protein 5 g, Fat 4 g, Carbohydrate 3 g, Fiber 1 g, Calcium 112 mg, Sodium 217 mg

CRANBERRY CHUTNEY

Yield: 6 to 8 servings

If you are one of those who refuses to eat canned cranberry sauce, you will enjoy this holiday favorite.

1 cup orange juice

One 12-ounce bag fresh cranberries, rinsed and stems removed

1 tablespoon fresh ginger, grated and chopped

1 cinnamon stick

½ cup Sucanat or other sweetener of choice

2 tablespoons arrowroot

¼ cup water

½ cup raisins (optional)

Pinch of cayenne pepper (optional)

Per serving: Calories 122, Protein 0 g, Fat 0 g, Carbohydrate 30 g, Fiber 2 g, Calcium 8 mg, Sodium 2 mg

1 Combine the orange juice, cranberries, ginger, and cinnamon stick in a saucepan, and boil on medium heat for about 12 to 15 minutes until the cranberries are tender and burst apart somewhat from boiling.

2 Strain the cranberries and set aside, reserving the liquid back into the saucepan.

3 Add the Sucanat and simmer for a few minutes until dissolved. Adjust the sweetness to taste. Do not be concerned if it seems extra sweet to you. The flavor will mellow once the cranberries are folded back into the sauce.

4 Dissolve the arrowroot and water together, and whip into the simmering sauce until thickened. Add the raisins and cayenne if desired.

5 Place the strained cranberries into a serving dish, and fold in the thickened sauce. Refrigerate the mixture until well chilled.

Hickory-Smoked Barbecue Sauce

Yield: 3 cups

Most barbecue sauces are sweetened with corn syrup or molasses, which contain at least 80% sugar. (Corn syrup has been linked to the onset of diabetes.) We use organic brown rice syrup as the sweetener. It contains only 20% natural sugar. This sauce can transform thinly sliced seitan (a wheat gluten product that resembles meat in texture) into a barbecue beef–style dish. Toss the sliced seitan with some of the sauce, and serve hot or cold with a sliced scallion garnish. You can also use it on grilled tofu steaks, tempeh, or veggie burgers. The vegetarian red chili paste used below is available in the Oriental foods section of most supermarkets.

16 ounces tomato purée

¾ cup brown rice syrup

½ teaspoon vegetarian red chili paste or any other of your favorite hot sauces

⅓ cup vegetarian Worcestershire sauce

¼ cup apple cider vinegar

1 teaspoon minced garlic

½ teaspoon liquid smoke

1 In a saucepan, simmer the tomato purée and brown rice syrup.

2 Dissolve the chili paste in a bowl with the remaining ingredients.

3 Fold the chili paste mixture into the tomato sauce, simmer, and stir from time to time.

Per ¼ cup: Calories 86, Protein 1 g, Fat 0 g, Carbohydrate 20 g, Fiber 1 g, Calcium 9 mg, Sodium 269 mg

Mango Duck Sauce

Yield: approximately 1½ cups

Mangoes are now available year round. Choose ripe ones that are soft to the touch. Serve this spicy sauce with vegetable spring rolls or other Oriental favorites.

1 large mango, peeled and sliced

¼ fresh pineapple, peeled, cored, and cut into chunks

½ cup brown rice vinegar

2 tablespoons brown rice syrup

2 teaspoons grated fresh ginger

2 teaspoons umeboshi plum vinegar (available in Oriental groceries and most natural food stores)

½ teaspoon vegetarian chili paste (available in the Oriental foods section of most supermarkets)

Per tablespoon: Calories 16, Protein 0 g, Fat 0 g, Carbohydrate 3 g, Fiber 0 g, Calcium 2 mg, Sodium 0 mg

1 Place all the ingredients in a blender, and purée thoroughly.

Marinara Sauce

This is my favorite marinara recipe. Organic tomatoes definitely enhance this sauce. To reduce fat calories, steps 1 and 2 can be omitted. Place all the ingredients in a large pot, cover, and simmer. For additional variety and flavor, you may add sliced domestic or wild mushrooms. To make a Bolognese–style meat sauce without the ground beef, add 12 ounces Boca Ground Burger and continue to cook for about 15 minutes before serving.

1 tablespoon extra-virgin olive oil (optional)

1 large yellow onion, chopped

2 tablespoons minced garlic

1 yellow bell pepper, chopped

1 red bell pepper, chopped

4 vine-ripe tomatoes, diced, or one 24-ounce can diced tomatoes

One 16-ounce can tomato purée

2 tablespoons finely chopped fresh oregano

2 tablespoons chopped fresh basil

2 bay leaves

¼ teaspoon cayenne pepper

½ teaspoon sea salt (optional)

⅓ cup brown rice syrup (optional— may be added if the sauce is too acidic in flavor)

1 Heat the olive oil in a heavy nonaluminum saucepan. Add the onion and garlic, and brown slightly.

2 Add the peppers and continue to cook until tender.

3 Add remaining ingredients, reduce the heat, and simmer for 1 hour or more, stirring frequently.

4 Adjust the seasonings to taste.

Per ½ cup: Calories 26, Protein 1 g, Fat 0 g, Carbohydrate 5 g, Fiber 1 g, Calcium 10 mg, Sodium 16 mg

Mexican Salsa

Yield: approximately 1 quart

This fat-free salsa can be used with Mexican entrees, for hors d'oeuvres, or as a salad dressing. For best quality use this within 3 days. For a more intensely flavored salsa, try roasting the peppers first. Remove the charred skin and dice before adding.

4 large vine-ripe tomatoes, chopped

1 Vidalia or red onion, chopped

1 yellow or orange bell pepper, chopped

1 jalapeño pepper, seeded and finely chopped (for note on handling hot peppers, see page 12)

1 teaspoon apple cider vinegar

2 tablespoons finely chopped fresh cilantro

2 teaspoons minced garlic

¼ teaspoon sea salt (optional)

1 Combine all the ingredients in a stainless steel bowl, and chill before serving. Adjust the spices as desired.

Per tablespoon: Calories 3, Protein 0 g, Fat 0 g, Carbohydrate 1 g, Fiber 0 g, Calcium 1 mg, Sodium 5 mg

Mock Bearnaise Sauce

This remake of the classic, but high-calorie, version is similar in color, flavor, and texture.

1 cup soymilk

4 tablespoons fresh lemon juice

2 teaspoons chopped fresh tarragon leaves

¼ teaspoon sea salt

½ teaspoon turmeric

Dash of cayenne pepper

2 tablespoons arrowroot

¼ cup distilled or pure water

1 Combine all the ingredients, except the arrowroot and water, in a saucepan, and bring to scalding.

2 Blend together the arrowroot and water, and whip into the sauce until thickened.

3 Adjust the seasonings to taste, cover, and set aside. Reheat when needed.

Per ¼ cup: Calories 26, Protein 1 g, Fat 0 g, Carbohydrate 4 g, Fiber 1 g, Calcium 3 mg, Sodium 94 mg

Pesto Sauce

Yield: 1½ cups

This sauce is wonderful over salads, vegetables, toasted whole grain breads, or with your favorite pasta. It will keep in the refrigerator for up to a month. For a more tropical or Southwestern flare, replace the basil with cilantro. You can also replace the basil with parsley for another flavor alternative.

¾ cup extra-virgin olive oil

2 teaspoons minced garlic

2 tablespoons chopped walnuts or pine nuts

⅛ teaspoon sea salt (optional)

⅓ cup soy or rice Parmesan

1 cup chopped fresh basil

Per tablespoon: Calories 68, Protein 1 g, Fat 7 g, Carbohydrate 0 g, Fiber 0 g, Calcium 1 mg, Sodium 29 mg

1 Combine all the ingredients in a blender, and purée thoroughly.

Savory Gravy

This sauce goes well with bread dressings, "Turkey–Style Tofu," page 136, or mashed potatoes. For a heartier gravy, add 8 ounces of sliced domestic or wild mushrooms.

1½ quarts pure or distilled water with vegetable broth powder added, to taste

1 tablespoon poultry seasoning

¼ teaspoon cayenne pepper

2 Vidalia or yellow onions, chopped

4 celery stalks, cut into ½-inch slices

⅔ cup arrowroot or kuzu

⅔ cup cool pure or distilled water

Per ¼ cup: Calories 59, Protein 0 g, Fat 0 g, Carbohydrate 14 g, Fiber 1 g, Calcium 17 mg, Sodium 21 mg

1 Bring the broth to a boil, and add all the ingredients.

2 Cook until the vegetables are tender. Strain out the vegetables, reserving the broth in a saucepan.

3 Return the broth to a boil, dissolve the arrowroot in the cool water, and whip into the broth until it reaches the desired thickness.

4 Return the vegetables to the sauce, adjust the seasonings to taste, and serve. Cover to avoid a skin forming on the top.

Stewed Tomatoes

Yield: 4 to 6 servings

My mother Ann is the inspiration for this dish. She would serve it over mashed potatoes or with steamed cabbage. Stewed tomatoes are more nutritious when combined with steamed fresh okra, cabbage, corn, green beans, Brussels sprouts, or like my mom does with mashed potatoes.

2 teaspoons extra-virgin olive oil

1 large yellow onion, chopped

1 yellow bell pepper, chopped

1 red bell pepper, chopped

1 tablespoon minced garlic

4 vine-ripe tomatoes, chopped, or one 16-ounce can diced tomatoes

⅔ cup tomato purée

½ cup brown rice syrup

2 tablespoons finely chopped fresh basil

2 bay leaves

½ teaspoon sea salt (optional)

Dash of cayenne pepper

Per serving: Calories 175, Protein 2 g, Fat 1 g, Carbohydrate 37 g, Fiber 3 g, Calcium 23 mg, Sodium 25 mg

1 Heat the olive oil in a heavy saucepan. Sauté the onion, peppers, and garlic.

2 When the vegetables have softened, add all the other ingredients. Simmer for 1 hour or more, stirring frequently.

3 Adjust the seasonings to taste. If you would like to eliminate the fat calories, do not use oil to sauté. Simply place all the other ingredients in a large pot, and cook slowly.

Sun-dried Tomato Tapenade

Yield: 1 cup

You can spread this over your favorite multi-grain bread, pasta, or vegetables as a more nutritious alternative to butter. This sauce will keep for over 1 month once refrigerated. To use again, return to room temperature before serving. For added variety and flavor, try adding 2 tablespoons chopped imported olives. You can also delete the sea salt from this recipe because the olives are salty.

½ cup extra-virgin olive oil

1½ teaspoons minced garlic

1 tablespoon chopped fresh basil

⅛ teaspoon sea salt (optional)

¼ cup sun-dried tomatoes, softened in hot water and coarsely chopped

1 Place the ingredients in a blender or food processor, and pulse a few times to purée.

Per tablespoon: Calories 61, Protein 0 g, Fat 7 g, Carbohydrate 0 g, Fiber 0 g, Calcium 0 mg, Sodium 1 mg

Teriyaki Glaze

Yield: approximately 3 cups

This sauce was developed for stir-fry vegetables or as a glaze for grilled foods such as tofu steaks or seitan slices.

1 cup water

⅔ cup apple or pineapple juice

⅔ cup brown rice syrup or other liquid sweetener

⅔ cup low-sodium tamari or soy sauce

⅓ cup unsweetened coconut flakes

2 tablespoons toasted sesame seeds

2 tablespoons minced garlic

1 tablespoon toasted sesame oil

1 tablespoon grated fresh ginger

1 teaspoon vegetarian chili paste, other hot sauce, or freshly ground black pepper

½ cup arrowroot combined with ½ cup cool water

Per 2 tablespoons: Calories 66, Protein 1 g, Fat 2 g, Carbohydrate 11 g, Fiber 0 g, Calcium 6 mg, Sodium 252 mg

1 Place everything but the arrowroot mixture in a saucepan, and bring to a slow boil.

2 Adjust the flavors to taste.

3 Slowly drizzle the arrowroot mixture into the boiling sauce. It should thicken immediately. Lower the flame and simmer for about 1 minute. If you need the sauce to be thicker, whip in some more water and arrowroot. If you would like the sauce thinner, add some fruit juice or water.

TOFU RICOTTA CHEESE ALTERNATIVE

Yield: approximately 2½ cups

For you Italian food lovers, do not despair. Here is a delicious cholesterol–free alternative to one of the staple ingredients in Italian cuisine—ricotta cheese. Use this in lasagne, manicotti, ravioli, eggplant Parmesan, eggplant rollatini, stuffed shells, and even the Greek specialty moussaka. You can also fold some sliced spinach leaves into the tofu mixture for additional nutrition and color.

1 pound firm or extra-firm tofu, pressed dry

2 tablespoons white or yellow miso

2 tablespoons tahini

2 ounces soy mozzarella, shredded

Per ¼ cup: Calories 72, Protein 5 g, Fat 3 g, Carbohydrate 3 g, Fiber 1 g, Calcium 103 mg, Sodium 52 mg

1 Cut the pressed tofu into 1 to 2-inch squares. Place in a food processor with the remaining ingredients, and purée. Scrape down the processor container, and purée again.

2 Remove the tofu from the processor with a rubber spatula, and use in your favorite recipe.

WILD MUSHROOM SAUCE

Yield: approximately 3 cups

This versatile sauce can also be served as a soup.

1 teaspoon canola or peanut oil

1 Vidalia or yellow onion, chopped

2 teaspoons minced garlic

2 cups portobello, shiitake, cremini, trumpet, or morel mushrooms, destemmed and sliced, or button mushrooms, sliced with the stems on

⅓ cup white or red wine

⅓ cup chopped sun-dried tomatoes (optional)

1 cup pure or distilled water

1 tablespoon tamari, or 1½ tablespoons Bragg Liquid Aminos

2 tablespoons chopped fresh basil, tarragon, or parsley

Dash of cayenne pepper

2 tablespoons arrowroot

1 In a saucepan, heat the oil and sauté the onion and garlic until lightly brown.

2 Add the mushrooms, wine, and sun-dried tomatoes, and cook until tender.

3 Add the water and spices to the vegetables, and simmer about 15 minutes, stirring occasionally.

4 Combine the arrowroot with ¼ cup cool water, whip it into the sauce, and simmer until the sauce has thickened.

5 Adjust the spices as desired, and serve.

Per ¼ cup: Calories 32, Protein 1 g, Fat 0 g, Carbohydrate 6 g, Fiber 0 g, Calcium 4 mg, Sodium 85 mg

Soups

Bavarian Lentil Soup

Yield: 4 to 6 servings

This is a nice hearty soup, high in protein, and could also serve as an entree.

3 quarts distilled or pure water

1 pound green or red lentils

1 large Vidalia or other yellow onion, chopped

2 carrots, diced

3 stalks celery, diced

2 bay leaves

2 tablespoons minced garlic

2 tablespoons Bragg Liquid Aminos

2 teaspoons curry powder

⅛ teaspoon cayenne pepper

Tofu hot dog slices or cooked brown rice, for garnish

Per serving: Calories 137, Protein 9 g, Fat 0 g, Carbohydrate 25 g, Fiber 4 g, Calcium 42 mg, Sodium 298 mg

1 In a large pot, bring the water to a boil. In a strainer, rinse the lentils, checking for stones.

2 Add the lentils, cover, and simmer for about 30 minutes, stirring occasionally.

3 Skim the foam off the stock, and add the vegetables and spices.

4 Continue to cook, skimming the foam as needed and stirring often to avoid scorching.

5 When the lentils are mushy and the soup has thickened as a result, adjust the spices to taste and serve. Garnish with sliced tofu hot dogs or cooked brown rice.

BLACK BEAN SOUP

Yield: 4 to 6 servings

What would a South Florida cookbook be without a black bean soup recipe? This recipe is also a lower-fat version of the Cuban classic. If there are leftovers, do not despair. You can drain the beans and follow the recipe for Black Bean and Corn Relish, page 14, or you may remove the bay leaf and purée to make a low-fat Black Bean Hummus, page 15. For complete protein, you may also combine it with brown rice to make black beans and rice. How is that for effective use of leftovers?

2½ quarts distilled or pure water

1 pound black beans

2 bay leaves

One 2-inch piece kombu, or 1 teaspoon kombu flakes

1 large yellow onion (Save a little for garnish.)

1 red bell pepper

3 tablespoons Bragg Liquid Aminos

2 tablespoons minced garlic

2 tablespoons ground cumin

2 tablespoons finely chopped fresh cilantro (Save a little for garnish.)

¼ teaspoon cayenne pepper

1 teaspoon sea salt (optional)

Per serving: Calories 134, Protein 7 g, Fat 0 g, Carbohydrate 25 g, Fiber 5 g, Calcium 34 mg, Sodium 2 mg

1 Soak the black beans in enough scalding water to cover for 2 hours or more.

2 Bring the distilled water to a boil. Drain the black beans and add to the boiling water with the bay leaves and kombu. Cook for 1 hour.

3 Chop the onion and bell pepper. Add them and the remaining ingredients to the beans, and cook until tender, about 30 minutes more.

4 Adjust the seasonings to taste, and garnish with diced onion and cilantro.

5 For a creamier texture, remove the bay leaf and place several cups of the soup in a blender. Remove the center of the blender top, and cover with a folded kitchen towel to allow steam to escape safely while blending. Purée the soup in batches until smooth.

CREAM OF BROCCOLI SOUP

Yield: 6 to 8 servings

The cream soups in this chapter are thickened with potatoes and whatever the main vegetable is in the recipe. Say good–bye to the flour, butter, and cream you find in most cream–style soups (as well as the cholesterol and fats that go along with them). For variety, add grated soy cheddar, Jack or mozzarella before serving. Try substituting celery, mushrooms, cauliflower, asparagus, or other favorite vegetable for the broccoli.

1 quart distilled or pure water

1 large yellow onion, sliced

3 Idaho potatoes, peeled and quartered

1 head broccoli

2 teaspoons minced garlic

⅛ teaspoon cayenne pepper

½ teaspoon sea salt (optional) or 1 tablespoon white or yellow miso

2 cups rice milk or soymilk

Per serving: Calories 94, Protein 3 g, Fat 1 g, Carbohydrate 17 g, Fiber 4 g, Calcium 37 mg, Sodium 26 mg

1 Bring the water to a boil. Add the onion and potatoes, and simmer until the potatoes are tender, about 20 minutes.

2 Remove the leaves and bottom half of the broccoli stalk, and cut the florettes and upper stem into 1½-inch pieces. Add to the stock with the garlic and spices, and cook until just tender. (Do not overcook the broccoli, or it will turn the soup to a brownish color.)

3 When the broccoli is tender, add the rice milk and remove from the heat.

4 Place several cups of the soup in a blender or food processor, and purée. (If you use a blender, remove the center of the blender top and cover with a folded kitchen towel to protect from steam build-up during processing.) Set aside in a large bowl. Purée the remaining soup in batches. Return to the pot and season to taste.

5 To serve, reheat the soup slowly to the desired temperature. Boiling the soup may cause it to curdle.

CREAM OF CARROT SOUP WITH DILL

Yield: 6 to 8 servings

To a large degree, the sweetness of the carrots will be responsible for the character of this soup.

1½ quarts distilled or pure water

1 pound carrots, scrubbed and cut into chunks

1 sweet potato, peeled and sliced

1 Vidalia or other onion, peeled and quartered

¼ teaspoon ground nutmeg

½ teaspoon ground cinnamon

Dash of cayenne pepper

1 cup rice milk or soymilk

1 tablespoon chopped fresh dill

½ teaspoon sea salt (optional)

Per serving: Calories 145, Protein 3 g, Fat 1 g, Carbohydrate 31 g, Fiber 6 g, Calcium 44 mg, Sodium 39 mg

1 Bring the water to a boil, and add the carrots, sweet potato, onion, nutmeg, cinnamon, and cayenne.

2 Simmer until the carrots are tender, then add the rice milk.

3 Purée several cups of the vegetable mix in a blender, taking care to remove the center of the blender top and cover with a folded kitchen towel to protect from steam build-up during processing. Place in a separate bowl, and purée the remaining mix, then return all the purée to the pot.

4 Reduce the heat to low, and fold in the fresh dill. Adjust the seasonings to taste, and serve hot or cold.

CREAM OF PLANTAIN SOUP

Yield: 6 to 8 servings

This success and sweetness of this delicious Caribbean banana soup will depend on your ability to pick the ripest plantains you can find. Do not be afraid if the plantains have black spots on them—they will be sweeter as a result. If the plantains are too green, allow to fully ripen for a few days before using. The plantain is a very nutritious vegetable. Do not be put off by its starchiness.

If you really want to add a hearty touch to this soup, as my assistant Andre did, add some Caribbean root vegetables, such as diced, steamed yuca, boniato, or malanga, and simmer for another 15 minutes to combine the flavors. It will be a meal in itself.

3 very ripe plantains, peeled and cut into 1-inch slices

1 teaspoon olive oil

1 Vidalia or yellow onion, chopped

1 tablespoon minced garlic

1 quart vegetable broth or water

1 cup vanilla soymilk

2 tablespoons yellow miso

Dash of cayenne pepper

1 tablespoon chopped cilantro

Per serving: Calories 128, Protein 2 g, Fat 2 g, Carbohydrate 26 g, Fiber 3 g, Calcium 13 mg, Sodium 8 mg

1 In a large saucepan, heat the olive oil, and sauté the onions until light brown; do not burn. Add the garlic and continue to cook.

2 Place the broth or water and plantains in the pan; cover and simmer until the plantains are tender.

3 Add the soymilk, miso, and cayenne, and simmer until hot.

4 Purée the mixture until creamy with a hand blender or in batches in a blender.

5 Return the purée to the pot, add the cilantro, adjust the seasonings to taste, and serve.

Fabulous 5-Bean Soup

Yield: 6 to 8 servings

This entree–style soup is truly a meal in itself. No need to make dinner if this soup is in your menu plans. It is so good that most guests request a second helping.

3 quarts distilled or pure water

½ cup chick-peas

½ cup kidney beans

½ cup lima beans

½ cup navy or Great Northern beans

½ cup black beans

2 bay leaves

1 large yellow onion, chopped

2 carrots, chopped

2 stalks celery, chopped

One 16-ounce can diced tomatoes

2 tablespoons minced garlic

2 tablespoons chopped fresh thyme

2 tablespoons chopped fresh basil

1 tablespoon chopped fresh oregano

⅛ teaspoon cayenne pepper

2 tablespoons Bragg Liquid Aminos

Per serving: Calories 191, Protein 11 g, Fat 1 g, Carbohydrate 35 g, Fiber 8 g, Calcium 64 mg, Sodium 209 mg

1 Soak the various types of beans separately in enough scalding water to cover for 1 to 2 hours.

2 Bring the distilled water to a boil in a large pot. Drain the chick-peas and kidney beans, add to the boiling water with the bay leaves, and cook for 30 minutes.

3 Drain the remaining soaked beans, add to the pot, and cook for 30 minutes.

4 Add the onions, carrots, celery, and tomatoes to the beans, and cook for 30 minutes, stirring occasionally.

5 Add the garlic and spices, lower the heat, and simmer for 30 minutes, or until the beans are tender.

6 Adjust the seasonings to taste. If the soup is too thick for your liking, add more water.

French Onion Soup

Yield: 4 servings

This recipe will rival any of your favorite onion soup recipes found in the finest restaurants. However, this one is also free of butter, dairy cheeses, animal–based broths, and the enriched flour that is used to thicken the soup.

1 tablespoon canola oil

3 large yellow onions, sliced ¼ inch thick

3 tablespoons whole wheat flour

1½ quarts distilled or pure water

1 large bay leaf

2 tablespoons vegetable protein soup base or low-sodium tamari

1 teaspoon sea salt (optional)

Dash of cayenne pepper

Per serving: Calories 95, Protein 3 g, Fat 2 g, Carbohydrate 13 g, Fiber 2 g, Calcium 32 mg, Sodium 303 mg

1 Heat the oil over medium-high heat in a large pot with a wide base. Add the onions, but do not stir until they are well-browned on one side. You must resist the urge to stir the onions before they brown. This caramelization process will add to the sweetness, as well as the color, of the soup. Once browned, stir and continue cooking.

2 When the onions have browned evenly, lower the heat and stir in the whole wheat flour. You must sprinkle the flour slowly to avoid lumps in the soup.

3 Raise the heat to medium-high, and stir in the water with a whip.

4 Add the remaining ingredients, reduce the heat until just simmering, and stir occasionally for 20 to 30 minutes. Adjust the spices to taste. Serve as is or with a slice of toasted wheat bread that has a slice of soy mozzarella melted on top.

Gazpacho

Yield: 4 to 6 servings

This spicy cold tomato soup is always better in the summer, when those backyard beefsteak tomatoes are ripe for the picking. If you like a little crunch to your soup, try Pita Croutons, page 96.

6 vine-ripe tomatoes, cored and quartered

1 small red onion, peeled and quartered

1 red bell pepper, seeds removed and quartered

1 tablespoon chopped fresh cilantro

⅓ cup balsamic vinegar

1 tablespoon chopped garlic

¼ cup olive oil

¼ teaspoon sea salt, or 2 teaspoons red miso

1 jalapeño pepper, seeds removed and chopped (for note on handling hot peppers, see page 12)

Garnishes

1 yellow bell pepper, chopped

1 large cucumber, peeled and chopped

1 small red onion, chopped

1 tablespoon chopped cilantro

Per serving: Calories 138, Protein 1 g, Fat 9 g, Carbohydrate 9 g, Fiber 3 g, Calcium 17 mg, Sodium 169 mg

1 Place all the ingredients, except the garnishes, in a blender or food processor, and purée. Adjust the seasonings to taste, and refrigerate until well chilled.

2 Toss all the garnishes together. Pour the soup into well-chilled soup bowls, and top with the garnish mix.

Island Gumbo Soup

Yield: 8-10 servings

This New Orleans specialty is hearty, spicy, and a meal in itself. The gumbo filé powder used here is ground sassafras leaves, used to thicken Creole dishes.

2 quarts vegetable broth or water

One 16-ounce can diced tomatoes

1 large yellow onion, chopped

2 red, orange, or yellow bell peppers, chopped

3 stalks celery, cut into ½-inch slices

2 tablespoons minced garlic

2 bay leaves

1 cup brown rice

2 tablespoons Cajun spice

2 teaspoons sea salt (optional)

2 cups sliced okra, fresh or frozen

2 tablespoons gumbo filé powder

Per serving: Calories 120, Protein 3 g, Fat 0 g, Carbohydrate 25 g, Fiber 4 g, Calcium 63 mg, Sodium 28 mg

1 Place the broth or water and tomatoes in a large pot, and bring to a boil.

2 Add the onion, peppers, celery, garlic, and bay leaf, bring back to a boil, and simmer for 15 minutes.

3 Add the brown rice and simmer about 30 minutes until tender.

4 Add the spice, salt, and okra. Cover and simmer 8 to 10 minutes until the okra is tender.

5 Remove from the heat and whip in the filé. (Do not add while the soup is simmering, or the filé will get stringy.) Adjust the seasonings to taste, and add more liquid if necessary to achieve the consistency you want.

LIMA BEAN SOUP

Yield: 4 to 6 servings

This is one of our most requested soups. Try using other white beans, such as navy or Great Northern, or combine all three.

2½ quarts distilled or pure water

1 pound lima beans or any other white beans

2 bay leaves

2 tablespoons minced garlic

1 large yellow onion, chopped

1 yellow or orange bell pepper, chopped

2 carrots, diced

One 12-ounce can diced tomatoes (optional)

1 tablespoon chopped fresh basil

Dash of cayenne pepper

2 teaspoons sea salt (optional)

Grilled tofu sausage (optional garnish)

Per serving: Calories 155, Protein 7 g, Fat 0 g, Carbohydrate 30 g, Fiber 7 g, Calcium 47 mg, Sodium 19 mg

1 Soak the beans in enough scalding water to cover for 1 to 2 hours.

2 Bring the distilled water to a boil. Drain the beans and add to the boiling water along with the bay leaves. Cook for 1 hour, skimming the foam from the surface of the simmering water.

3 Add the remaining ingredients, and cook for about 1 hour, or until the beans are tender.

4 Adjust the seasonings to taste, and garnish with grilled tofu sausage.

5 For a creamier texture, remove the bay leaf and place several cups of the soup in a blender. Remove the center of the blender top, and cover with a folded kitchen towel to protect from steam build-up during processing. Purée the soup in batches until smooth.

BLACK AND WHITE BEAN SOUP

Purée Lima Bean Soup (without the tomatoes) and Black Bean Soup, page 73, separately in a blender. Place a soup bowl between the two pots of soup. With a ladle of the same size in each hand, ladle the soups into opposite sides of the bowl at the same time. (See photo opposite page 33.)

Mexican Tortilla Soup

Tomatillos are Mexican green tomatoes, small and pungent in flavor. They are not an unripened tomato, but are green at harvest and will stay that color throughout. This flavorful soup is a perfect start to a Mexican theme lunch or dinner.

For a smokier flavor, try roasting the peppers, page 205, and cut before adding to the soup. You can also roast the corn on the cob. Wet the husk with cool water, wrap in foil, and bake or broil on the grill for 35 to 40 minutes. Unwrap, allow to cool, and you will be amazed at how easy the husk comes off.

1 tablespoon canola or olive oil

1 large Vidalia or yellow onion, chopped

1 tablespoon minced garlic

1 yellow bell pepper, chopped

1 red bell pepper, chopped

1 large jalapeño pepper, finely chopped (for note on handling hot peppers, see page 12)

2 vine-ripe tomatoes, chopped or one 16-ounce can diced tomatoes

6 tomatillos, chopped (optional)

1½ quarts vegetable broth, or pure or distilled water

¼ cup lite tamari or soy sauce

1 Heat the olive oil in a large pot, and sauté the onions and garlic.

2 Add the peppers, tomatoes, and tomatillos, and simmer for 10 to 15 minutes.

3 Add the broth, tamari, bay leaf, cumin, and corn, and continue to cook for 20 minutes.

1 bay leaf

1 teaspoon ground cumin

4 ears corn, cut from the cob, or
1 cup frozen cut corn

3 yellow or blue corn tortillas, cut
in half and then cut into
¼-inch strips

1 teaspoon chopped fresh oregano

2 tablespoons chopped fresh
cilantro or basil

Per serving: Calories 127, Protein 4 g,
Fat 3 g, Carbohydrate 20 g, Fiber 4 g,
Calcium 42 mg, Sodium 513 mg

4 While the soup is cooking, preheat the oven to 400°F. Spread
the cut tortillas on a baking
sheet, and bake for 25 to 30 minutes until lightly golden browned
and crispy. Turn the tortillas over
after 15 minutes for even baking.

5 Add the fresh herbs to the soup,
adjust the spices to taste, and
serve hot with the crispy tortilla
chips as a garnish.

Minestrone

Yield: 6 to 8 servings

This Italian specialty can be served as an appetizer or main course.

3 quarts distilled or pure water

½ cup dry kidney beans, or 1 cup cooked

½ cup dry chick-peas, or 1 cup cooked

1 large yellow onion, chopped

2 carrots, chopped

2 stalks celery, chopped

1 red bell pepper, chopped

2 bay leaves

1 tablespoon minced garlic

3 vine-ripe tomatoes, or 3 cups diced tomatoes

2 tablespoons chopped fresh oregano

2 tablespoons chopped fresh basil

Dash of cayenne pepper

2 tablespoons Bragg Liquid Aminos

1 cup macaroni

4 ounces fresh spinach, rinsed, stems removed, and chopped (about 1½ cups)

Per serving: Calories 153, Protein 7 g, Fat 0 g, Carbohydrate 29 g, Fiber 5 g, Calcium 57 mg, Sodium 226 mg

1 If using dry beans, soak them in enough scalding water to cover for 1 to 2 hours. Bring the distilled water to a boil. Strain the beans, add to the boiling water, and cook for 1 hour. If using cooked beans, add them with the tomatoes in step 4.

2 Add the onion, carrots, celery, bell pepper, bay leaves, and garlic to the cooking beans (or boiling water), and simmer for 1 hour.

3 Add the tomatoes, herbs, pepper, Bragg, (and cooked beans, if using) and cook until the beans are tender.

4 Adjust the seasonings to taste, add the macaroni and cook about 8 to 10 minutes. (At this point you may need to add a little water or vegetable stock if the soup is too thick.)

5 About 5 minutes before serving, add the spinach. Cover and simmer for 5 minutes, and serve.

Miso Soup

Miso is one of the oldest condiments known to man. It is somewhat salty, with a smooth texture like creamy peanut butter. Miso comes in many varieties. You can find light or dark barley miso, red soybean miso, chick-pea miso, and miso of many other colors and flavors. It's a fresh food with lots of natural enzymes, so don't boil it—add it to your hot broth and serve within a few minutes to take advantage of its many nutritional benefits.

For a more nutritious and flavorful change, try adding ¼ cup of wakame (seaweed) slices to the broth at the same time as the carrots and proceed with the recipe. For added protein, we fold in 6 ounces of diced tofu just before serving.

5 cups pure or distilled water

4 ounces button or shiitake mushrooms, sliced ¼ inch thick

2 teaspoons minced garlic

2 tablespoons yellow or white miso (or your favorite variety)

1 carrot, cut into ⅛ x 1-inch julienne strips

3 scallions, sliced ¼ inch thick

1 teaspoon sesame oil

Per serving: Calories 39, Protein 1 g, Fat 1 g, Carbohydrate 5 g, Fiber 1 g, Calcium 9 mg, Sodium 321 mg

1 Bring the water to a boil in a 2- or 3-quart pan.

2 Add the mushrooms and garlic, and simmer until the mushrooms are tender.

3 Add the carrots, scallions, and sesame oil to the soup, and continue to simmer.

4 Remove about ½ cup of the broth to a small bowl, and whisk in the miso.

5 When the miso has dissolved, fold into the soup, adjust the seasonings to taste, and turn off the heat. To reheat, do not bring the soup to a boil.

Roasted Red Pepper Vichyssoise

Yield: 6 servings

This classical cold soup with a twist is also very good served hot.

3 large red bell peppers, cut into wide pieces for roasting

1 quart pure or distilled water or vegetable broth

3 large Idaho potatoes, peeled and cut into slices

1 Vidalia or yellow onion

1 tablespoon fresh minced garlic

1 cup rice milk or soymilk

2 tablespoons white miso, or ½ teaspoon sea salt

Dash of cayenne pepper

1 leek, split in half and thinly sliced, or ¼ cup sliced chives

Per serving: Calories 200, Protein 5 g, Fat 1 g, Carbohydrate 40 g, Fiber 6 g, Calcium 50 mg, Sodium 23 mg

1 Set the oven to broil at 500°F.

2 Place the sliced peppers skin side up on a lightly oiled cookie sheet. Place the pan on the top oven rack for about 15 minutes until the skin is charred. Remove the pan from the oven, and cover the peppers with a lid or another pan. Let the peppers steam for about 30 minutes, or until cool. Remove the charred skins and set aside the cleaned peppers for later. Be sure to rinse away the black pieces, as they could discolor the soup.

3 While the peppers are roasting, bring the water to a boil in a large pot. Add the potatoes, onion, and garlic. Simmer for about 20 minutes until the potatoes are tender.

4 Add the rice milk, miso, and cayenne, and simmer until hot.

5 Remove from the heat. Purée the potato mixture and the roasted red peppers in a blender until creamy. Return this purée to the pot.

6 Fold in the sliced leeks, adjust the seasoning as desired, and simmer about 3 minutes. Remove the pot from the stove, and chill the mixture in the refrigerator until cool. If you are in a hurry, place the soup in the freezer, and stir from time to time until cool.

MUSHROOM-BARLEY SOUP

Yield: 6 to 8 servings

This classic soup actually tastes better when the beef brisket is excluded.
For extra flavor, color and nutrition, try adding 3 ounces or 2 cups of fresh sliced spinach
five minutes before serving.

3 quarts distilled or pure water

1 large yellow onion, chopped

2 carrots, chopped

2 stalks celery, chopped

1 large bay leaf

1 cup barley

1 pound fresh mushrooms, sliced
   ¼-inch thick

1 tablespoon minced garlic

3 tablespoons Bragg Liquid Aminos

1 tablespoon coarsely chopped fresh
   basil

Dash of cayenne pepper

Per serving: Calories 103, Protein 4 g,
Fat 0 g, Carbohydrate 22 g, Fiber 4 g,
Calcium 28 mg, Sodium 321 mg

1 In a large pot, bring the water to a boil.

2 Add the onion, carrots, celery, bay leaf, and barley, and simmer for 20 minutes. Add half of the mushrooms, and cook for about 20 more minutes.

3 Add the remaining ingredients, and simmer for about 10 minutes. At this point the barley should be fully expanded. You may need to adjust the seasonings to taste if you add more water to thin the soup.

Split Pea Soup

This is an easy soup to prepare, with a fresh, distinctive flavor. If you want to add some sweetness and texture, try adding 2 cups of diced butternut squash to the soup about half an hour before it's finished cooking. Garnish with whole wheat pita croutons or tofu hot dogs, or serve with brown rice for a more complete protein.

3 quarts distilled or pure water

1 pound split peas

1 large Vidalia or yellow onion, chopped

2 carrots, diced

3 stalks celery, diced

2 bay leaves

2 teaspoons sea salt (optional)

Dash of cayenne pepper

Per serving: Calories 96, Protein 5 g, Fat 0 g, Carbohydrate 18 g, Fiber 5 g, Calcium 26 mg, Sodium 24 mg

1 In a large pot, bring the water to a boil. Rinse the peas in a strainer, removing any stones.

2 Add the peas to the pot, cover, and simmer for about 30 minutes, stirring occasionally.

3 Skim the foam off the surface of the simmering water, and add the vegetables and spices.

4 Continue to cook for about 1 hour, skimming the foam as needed and stirring often to avoid scorching the bottom of the pot.

5 When the peas are mushy and the soup has thickened as a result, adjust the spices to taste and serve.

Spring Vegetable Soup

Yield: 6 to 8 servings

Asparagus is now available year round, so this soup is no longer just meant for spring.

2 quarts distilled or pure water

1 large yellow onion

2 carrots, chopped

2 stalks celery, chopped

One 12-ounce can diced tomatoes

2 large bay leaves

1 tablespoon minced garlic

2 teaspoons sea salt (optional)

1 zucchini

1 yellow squash

8 ounces fresh asparagus

1 tablespoon coarsely chopped fresh basil

Dash of cayenne pepper

1. In a large pot, bring the water to a boil, and add the onion, carrots, celery, tomatoes, bay leaf, garlic, and salt. Simmer for about 20 minutes, until the carrots are tender.

2. Cut the zucchini and squash into 1-inch cubes. Add to the pot and cook for 15 minutes.

3. Slice the asparagus into 1-inch pieces, and add to the pot with the basil and cayenne; cover and simmer for 5 minutes.

4. Season to taste and serve as soon as the asparagus is tender.

Per serving: Calories 46, Protein 2 g, Fat 0 g, Carbohydrate 9 g, Fiber 3 g, Calcium 38 mg, Sodium 26 mg

VEGETABLE BROTH

Yield: approximately 1 gallon

This broth is a natural diuretic that can be used as a beverage or soup base.

1½ gallons distilled or pure water

3 large yellow onions, peeled and quartered

1 small head green cabbage

1 bunch celery with leaves, washed thoroughly and trimmed

1 pound whole carrots, scrubbed well

2 pounds white or red potatoes

1 bouquet garni (bundle of fresh herbs, peppercorns, garlic clove, and bay leaf—optional, for added flavor)

1 Combine all the ingredients in a large pot, and simmer for 2 hours or more. You may leave this stock on the stove over low heat for the better part of the day.

2 When finished, discard the vegetables and bouquet garni, and strain the stock. This will keep well in the refrigerator for 3 to 5 days. You may also freeze it for future use.

Winter Squash Soup

Yield: 4 servings

This soup is closer to a stew in texture and very flavorful.

3 acorn or butternut squash, cut in quarters and seeds removed

Cinnamon and nutmeg, for topping

1 teaspoon canola oil

1 large Vidalia or yellow onion, sliced

1 tablespoon minced garlic

1 cup vegetable broth

1 cup rice milk or soymilk

2 tablespoons yellow or white miso

One 12.3-ounce box firm silken tofu, broken into pieces

1 tablespoon chopped fresh rosemary

Dash of cayenne pepper

Per serving: Calories 228, Protein 10 g, Fat 5 g, Carbohydrate 35 g, Fiber 9 g, Calcium 132 mg, Sodium 46 mg

1 Place the squash skin side down in a casserole dish, and dust lightly with cinnamon and nutmeg. Cover with foil and bake at 400°F for 1 hour, or until tender. Remove from the oven and scoop out the pulp.

2 In a large saucepan, heat the oil and brown the onion and garlic.

3 Add the remaining ingredients and the squash, and simmer for about 20 minutes.

4 Purée the ingredients in a blender, adjust the seasonings to taste, and serve.

Breads
and
Sandwiches

FOCACCIA

Yield: Two 10-inch rounds (12 servings)

Focaccia is a flat and flavorful Italian bread, wonderful with a salad or dinner.

Dough

¾ cup pure or distilled water

2 teaspoons baking yeast

½ teaspoon sea salt

¾ cup whole wheat flour

¾ cup whole grain pastry flour

1 teaspoon chopped fresh thyme or
   rosemary

Per serving: Calories 67, Protein 2 g,
Fat 1 g, Carbohydrate 12 g, Fiber 1 g,
Calcium 18 mg, Sodium 90 mg

1 To make the dough, combine the water, baking yeast, and salt in a large bowl or mixer.

2 Combine the flours with the liquid until smooth, then fold in the 1 teaspoon thyme or rosemary.

3 Turn the mix onto a floured table, and knead for 2 to 3 minutes.

4 Place in an oiled bowl, cover, and let rise in a warm place for 1 hour or until the volume is almost doubled.

5 Preheat the oven to 375°F while the bread is resting.

Topping

1 tablespoon extra-virgin olive oil

1 Vidalia or yellow onion, peeled, halved, and cut into ¼-inch slices

1 teaspoon minced garlic

1 tablespoon chopped fresh rosemary

⅓ cup chopped sun-dried tomatoes (optional)

6 To make the topping, heat the oil, add the vegetables and herbs, and cook until tender. Set aside.

7 Place the dough on a lightly floured surface, and cut in half.

8 With a rolling pin, roll out the dough into two 8 to 10-inch circles. They do not have to be perfect.

9 Place them on a nonstick or lightly oiled baking sheet, sprinkle half of the topping over each circle, and let rise for 30 minutes. Bake for 18 to 20 minutes until the crust is lightly browned.

PITA CROUTONS

Yield: 1½ cups

The crunchiness of these croutons are habit forming. There are worse habits to have.

2 pieces whole wheat pita bread

1 tablespoon extra-virgin olive oil

1 teaspoon minced garlic

1 teaspoon dried oregano leaves

Per ¼ cup: Calories 70, Protein 2 g, Fat 3 g, Carbohydrate 9 g, Fiber 1 g, Calcium 20 mg, Sodium 107 mg

1 Preheat the oven to 400°F.

2 Cut the pita bread into ¾-inch squares, and set aside.

3 Whisk together the olive oil, garlic, and oregano.

4 Thoroughly toss the oil mixture with the pita. Spread the pita pieces evenly on a baking sheet.

5 Bake for 15 to 18 minutes, or until brown and crispy. Cool and serve with soy Parmesan over your favorite soup or salad. These are also very good as a snack!

Homemade breads are a delicious way to add the nutritional benefits of whole grains and seeds to your meals. Use whole wheat pitas with a variety of fillings, and try Focaccia, pp. 94–95, shown at top.

"Not So Sloppy Joes"

Yield: 6 to 8 servings

Using textured soy protein as a replacement for ground beef or turkey in this recipe will give a you a fat-free vegetarian alternative to this baby-boomer generation classic. Serve in a whole wheat pita as a sandwich, or over pasta, brown rice, or potatoes.

1 small yellow onion, diced

1 red or yellow bell pepper, diced

2 teaspoons minced garlic

1½ cups pure or distilled water or vegetable broth

1 cup fruit-sweetened low-sodium ketchup

2 tablespoons vegetarian Worcestershire sauce

1 teaspoon hot sauce

½ teaspoon liquid hickory smoke (optional)

¼ cup brown rice syrup

1¼ cups textured soy protein granules or 12 ounces Boca Ground Burger

1 Simmer the onion, pepper, and garlic in the water until tender.

2 Add the ketchup, Worcestershire sauce, hot sauce, liquid hickory smoke, and brown rice syrup; cover, and simmer.

3 Fold in the textured soy protein or ground burger, cover, and simmer for 15 to 20 minutes until tender.

4 Adjust the spices as desired. Add more liquid as needed.

Per serving: Calories 134, Protein 8 g, Fat 0 g, Carbohydrate 24 g, Fiber 2 g, Calcium 51 mg, Sodium 336 mg

Clockwise from top left: Portobello Mushroom Burger, p. 99, Tofu-Vegetable Lasagne, pp. 118–19, and Pasta with Pesto Sauce, Wild Mushrooms, and Sun-Dried Tomatoes, p. 106

Philly Seitan Steak 'n Cheese Sandwich

Yield: 4 servings

If you need to satisfy that chewy craving in minutes, here is one of our favorites. Personally, I would also lather some stone-ground mustard and an eggless mayonnaise spread on both sides of the roll.

1 teaspoon extra-virgin olive or canola oil

One 8-ounce package seitan pieces, your favorite flavor, thinly sliced

4 slices (3 ounces) soy mozzarella or cheddar

1 Vidalia or yellow onion, thinly sliced

2 whole grain hoagie rolls, cut half lengthwise

2 crisp romaine leaves (optional)

4 tomato slices (optional)

Per serving: Calories 326, Protein 27 g, Fat 5 g, Carbohydrate 44 g, Fiber 2 g, Calcium 162 mg, Sodium 425 mg

1 Heat the oil in a large sauté pan, and sauté the onions until lightly browned.

2 Fold in the seitan slices, and continue to cook until heated through.

3 Bunch the seitan and onions close together in the pan, and cover with the vegetarian cheese slices. Cover the pan and simmer until the cheese melts.

4 Serve on the hoagie rolls, and garnish as desired.

Portobello Mushroom Burger

Yield: 4 servings

The portobello mushroom is very large and has a meaty texture, making a great sandwich.

2 tablespoons extra-virgin olive oil

1 small red or yellow bell pepper

1 teaspoon minced garlic

1 teaspoon chopped fresh thyme or rosemary

Dash of cayenne pepper

4 portobello mushrooms, rinsed well and stems removed

4 whole grain rolls

4 romaine leaves

4 large vine-ripe tomato slices

1 red onion, thinly sliced

1 roasted yellow or red bell pepper, skinned and quartered

Per serving: Calories 209, Protein 7 g, Fat 7 g, Carbohydrate 31 g, Fiber 4 g, Calcium 64 mg, Sodium 250 mg

1 Preheat the barbecue grill on high. For added flavor, add some soaked mesquite chips.

2 In a blender, purée the olive oil, bell pepper, garlic, herbs, and cayenne.

3 With a small spoon, scoop out the gills on the undersides of the mushroom caps. Brush both sides of the mushrooms with the herb purée.

4 Grill the mushrooms until tender, 3 to 4 minutes on each side.

5 Preheat the oven to 400°F. Place the mushrooms in a casserole dish, cover, and bake for 15 minutes more.

6 Toast the buns and serve with the mushrooms, romaine, sliced tomatoes, onion, roasted pepper, and any of your favorite condiments.

VEGETARIAN DELI SANDWICHES IN MINUTES

This section is my tribute to my good friend and sandwich lover Julio Dilorio. He never ceased to come up with delicious sandwich combinations for my staff and I to make for him. To all those people out there that hate cooking, here are some quick and easy sandwich ideas. Most items can be purchased already presliced.

BARBECUE SEITAN

Yield: 3 to 4 servings

One 12-ounce package barbecue or chicken-style seitan pieces, thinly sliced

¼ cup Barbecue Sauce, page 59, or your favorite brand

½ teaspoon hot sauce

2 scallions, thinly sliced

1 Toss the seitan slices with the two sauces, and serve hot or cold in a whole wheat pita or roll, between slices of whole grain bread, or over brown rice or quinoa. Garnish with the sliced scallions.

Per serving: Calories 111, Protein 13 g, Fat 0 g, Carbohydrate 16 g, Fiber 7 g, Calcium 89 mg, Sodium 577 mg

QUICK SLOPPY JOES

Yield: 4 servings

This is the mega–fast version of the "Not So Sloppy Joes" on page 97. Serve as is, or in a bun or pita, over your favorite grains, or in a baked potato.

½ cup vegetable broth

⅔ cup fruit-sweetened low-sodium ketchup, or your favorite

1 tablespoon vegetarian Worcestershire sauce

½ teaspoon hot sauce

⅔ cup textured soy protein granules

1 Combine the broth, ketchup, vegetarian Worcestershire sauce, and hot sauce in a saucepan, and heat until bubbly. Add the textured soy granules, cover, and simmer about 5 minutes or until tender. Adjust the seasonings to taste, and serve.

Per serving: Calories 86, Protein 8 g, Fat 0 g, Carbohydrate 13 g, Fiber 1 g, Calcium 41 mg, Sodium 328 mg

Vegetarian Hamburger Helper

Once again we use textured soy protein to replace ground beef in recipes. It is high in protein, zinc, and other important nutrients and low in fat and calories. What else could you ask for in food? And it is also very inexpensive to buy. This dish is great served alone as a stew, but we like it better served over brown rice, quinoa, millet, pasta, or as a filling for a baked potato.

1 teaspoon canola or extra-virgin olive oil

1 Vidalia or yellow onion, chopped

1 to 2 tablespoons minced garlic

8 ounces mushrooms, sliced

2 tablespoons whole wheat pastry flour

2 cups vegetable broth, mushroom broth, or water

1 tablespoon Bragg Liquid Aminos, or 2 teaspoons low-sodium tamari

1½ cups textured soy protein granules

1 tablespoon chopped fresh thyme or basil

Dash of cayenne pepper, or 1 teaspoon hot sauce

1 cup frozen baby peas or cut corn, or a combination

1. Heat the oil in a large pot, and sauté the onions and garlic until lightly browned.

2. Add the mushrooms and simmer about 3 minutes until tender.

3. Lower the heat and sprinkle in the flour a little at a time.

4. Raise the heat, whisk in the vegetable broth and Bragg, and simmer until thickened.

5. Fold in the textured soy granules, thyme, and cayenne, and simmer for 8 to 10 minutes until the granules are tender.

6. Add the peas and/or corn, and simmer 3 minutes, adjust the seasonings to taste, and serve.

Per serving: Calories 208, Protein 22 g, Fat 2 g, Carbohydrate 25 g, Fiber 7 g, Calcium 111 mg, Sodium 268 mg

Vegetarian Roulade (wrap) Sandwich

Yield: 2 wraps (6 to 8 servings)

With the popularity of wrap sandwiches today, here is a colorful and nutritious sandwich that is as fun to make as it is to eat.

3 cups hummus (with roasted red peppers), page 16

1 pound spinach, cleaned and destemmed, or romaine lettuce leaves

3 vine-ripe tomatoes, cut into ¼-inch slices

8 ounces button mushrooms, cut into ⅛-inch slices

2 cups shredded carrots

2 cups alfalfa sprouts

2 soft, flat bread sheets (available in natural food stores) or tortillas

Per serving: Calories 239, Protein 8 g, Fat 8 g, Carbohydrate 35 g, Fiber 9 g, Calcium 145 mg, Sodium 206 mg

1 Prepare the hummus and vegetables, and organize for assembly.

2 Lay one of the bread sheets in front of you parallel to the edge of the counter.

3 Spread about 1½ cup of the hummus on the bread.

4 Arrange the spinach over the hummus.

5 Place a layer of each of the remaining items across the middle third of the bread.

6 To roll, grab the edge of the bread nearest to you with both hands, and begin to roll. You may need to tuck in the vegetables as you roll.

7 When the roll is complete, trim off the excess vegetables.

8 Cut the roll into 1-inch-thick slices, and serve with stone-ground mustard, creamy garlic dressing, or mustard tahini.

Pasta
Entrees

PASTA

Varieties and Cooking Methods

The popularity of pasta has never been greater than today. As a result, many of us eat pasta three or more times a week. For that reason I thought it would be helpful to present you with some important information that may help you make the right choice when selecting your pasta.

Our pasta of choice at the spa, and also in this book, is whole grain pasta that has not been enriched. There are many brands on the market that are excellent. The brand we have the most experience with is DeBoles. It is available in most grocery stores, as well as the majority of natural food stores. Deboles pasta comes in both traditional and nontraditional shapes and sizes. What separates DeBoles from most pastas is that the ingredients are very basic and wholesome, in many cases just whole wheat flour and Jerusalem artichoke flour. Deboles also has a semolina pasta, and for those who have an allergy to wheat gluten they also make a corn pasta. Their pastas are not enriched, unlike most commercial brands on the market. Due to the additional milling and processing involved in making commercial pasta flour, it has been stripped of its fiber and essential B vitamins. When you read the labels of enriched pastas, you will also see that the B vitamins riboflavin, niacin, folic acid and thiamine have had to be added to "re-enrich" the pastas, as I describe it. By consuming whole grain pastas, we are getting better nutritional value in the form of added protein and fiber, which results in better digestion of these foods.

There are many other whole grain pastas available in natural food stores. Quinoa pasta is wheat-free and comes from quinoa, one of the oldest grains known to man. It has a bright yellow color when cooked, which brings a unique appearance to any pasta presentation.

Lupinni pasta is made from the lupin bean. Rich in protein and somewhat hearty in flavor, this pasta is not starchy or sticky after cooking like other pastas are.

There are other whole grain pastas to choose from, such as amaranth, spelt, and rye pastas. Soba noodles are popular in Oriental cooking and are made either of buckwheat flour only or a combination of buckwheat and whole wheat flour. Once you have experienced these superior pastas, you will never go back to enriched pastas again.

Cooking pasta is rather simple. Let your water come to a boil, and follow the manufacturer's instructions for determining how long to cook it. Do not cook at a rolling boil, or you may cause the pasta to break apart. I no longer add salt or oil to the pasta-cooking water. If you have made a flavorful sauce to compliment the pasta, there is no need to add salt to the cooking water to bring out more flavor. Many cooks recommend using vegetable oil in the cooking water to keep pasta from sticking, but this method adds unnecessary fat grams to your food. I suggest pouring the pasta into a strainer after it has become as tender as you like it, and "shock" it with cold running water while stirring gently with a wooden spoon or rubber spatula. This stops the pasta from cooking any more and removes some of the starchiness as well. From time to time, splash the pasta in the strainer with cool water to avoid any sticking. Do not submerge your pasta in water for a long period of time. This will affect the palatability and texture. To reheat the pasta, simply dip the strainer into a pot of boiling water for a minute, shake off the excess water, toss with your heated sauce, and serve.

That's how all your favorite restaurants reheat their pasta—why should you do it any differently at home? This also allows you to cook your pasta before your sauce is ready and reheat it when needed.

Pasta with pesto sauce, wild mushrooms, and sun-dried tomatoes

Yield: 4 servings

This is one of our most requested entrees. Feel free to try other pasta varieties.

4 portobello mushrooms, and/or ½ pound shiitake mushrooms

3 ounces sun-dried tomatoes

12 ounces whole wheat or durum semolina angel hair pasta

1 teaspoon canola or olive oil

1 tablespoon minced garlic

2 teaspoons chopped fresh thyme

½ cup Pesto Sauce, page 64

¼ cup soy or rice Parmesan

Basil spring, for garnish

Per serving: Calories 409, Protein 18 g, Fat 18 g, Carbohydrate 47 g, Fiber 1 g, Calcium 12 mg, Sodium 240 mg

1 Remove the stems from the mushrooms. If you're using portobellos, scrape off the gills on the underside and slice ¼ inch thick. Cut the shiitakes in half.

2 Soften the sun-dried tomatoes, if necessary, in enough hot water to cover, then drain and slice ½ inch thick.

3 Bring a pot of water to a boil, and cook the pasta 4 to 5 minutes, or until al dente.

4 Strain the pasta, rinse with cool water, and set aside in a strainer.

5 Heat the oil in a medium pan, and add the garlic, mushrooms, and thyme. Cover and cook until tender. Drain off any liquid that has exuded from the mushrooms.

6 Reheat the pasta by quickly submerging the strainer in boiling water, then drain.

7 In a large serving bowl, add the pasta, drained mushrooms, sun-dried tomatoes, and pesto.

8 Serve hot and top with soy Parmesan and a basil sprig for garnish.

Pasta e Fagioli

In this vegetarian rendition, we have replaced the pancetta with tofu sausage—delish!

2 teaspoons olive oil

1 large Vidalia or yellow onion, diced

2 tablespoons minced garlic

One 12-ounce can diced tomatoes

1 quart pure or distilled water

1 cup dry navy or Great Northern beans, presoaked in scalding water for 2 hours

4 vegetarian Italian sausages, grilled and sliced

2 tablespoons chopped fresh basil

½ teaspoon sea salt (optional)

Dash of cayenne pepper

1 cup rigatoni or penne pasta

Per serving: Calories 231, Protein 12 g, Fat 4 g, Carbohydrate 36 g, Fiber 7 g, Calcium 73 mg, Sodium 145 mg

1 In a large soup pot, add the olive oil and heat to sauté. Add the onion and lightly brown.

2 Add the garlic and continue to cook for about 2 minutes. Add the tomatoes and simmer for 5 minutes.

3 Add the water and bring to a boil. Drain the soaked beans, add to the pot, and simmer for 45 minutes until tender.

4 Add the sausage slices, basil, salt, cayenne, and pasta and cook for 10 to 12 minutes until the pasta is tender.

5 Adjust the seasonings to taste, and serve with some grated soy Parmesan as a garnish.

BAKED ZITI WITH MEATLESS MARINARA SAUCE

Yield: 6 to 8 servings

It is very easy to duplicate this old favorite by using your favorite vegetarian burger substitute or textured soy protein granules. You may also try replacing the meat substitute with broccoli and mushrooms for variety.

Meatless Marinara Sauce

2 yellow onions, diced

1 tablespoon minced garlic

1 red bell pepper, diced

1 yellow bell pepper, diced

2 teaspoons extra-virgin olive oil

One 12-ounce can diced tomatoes, or 2 cups diced fresh tomatoes

One 12-ounce can tomato purée

2 tablespoons oregano (chopped fresh if available)

2 tablespoons chopped fresh basil

2 bay leaves

¼ teaspoon cayenne pepper

½ teaspoon sea salt (optional)

1 In a large pot over medium heat, sauté the onions, garlic, and peppers in the oil until the vegetables are tender.

2 Add the remaining ingredients, cover, and simmer for about 1 hour, stirring frequently. Adjust the seasonings to taste.

3 Add the ground burger or textured soy granules to the vegetables, and continue to cook, stirring occasionally, for 10 to 15 minutes until the burger or granules are tender.

12 ounces Boca Ground Burger,
  or 2 cups reconstituted textured
  soy protein granules

1 pound ziti

8 ounces soy mozzarella

Per serving: Calories 285, Protein 24 g,
Fat 7 g, Carbohydrate 36 g, Fiber 7 g,
Calcium 183 mg, Sodium 528 mg

4 Preheat the oven to 400°F. Cook the ziti according to the package directions; drain and set aside in a strainer.

5 In a large mixing bowl, fold together the meatless sauce and ziti.

6 Place the casserole mixture in a 10 x 13-inch baking dish, and top with the shredded cheese.

7 Bake until the cheese is slightly brown, and serve.

Fettuccine Carbonara

Yield: 3 to 4 servings

In another attempt to recreate a rather calorie–rich favorite of ours, we must find meatless alternatives for the bacon or ham, heavy cream, and butter. No small task, but you will be amazed at the finished product.

Alfredo Sauce

One 12.3-ounce box extra-firm or
   firm silken tofu

2 cups rice milk or soymilk

1 teaspoon minced garlic

¼ teaspoon sea salt (optional)

Dash of ground nutmeg

Dash of cayenne pepper,
   or ½ tea-spoon freshly ground
   black pepper

¾ cup soy or rice Parmesan

2 teaspoons chopped fresh basil

Per serving: Calories 504, Protein 39 g, Fat 15 g, Carbohydrate 53 g, Fiber 6 g, Calcium 87 mg, Sodium 991 mg

1 Place the silken tofu, rice milk, garlic, salt, nutmeg, cayenne, and Parmesan in a blender, and purée until creamy. Fold in the chopped basil. Heat the sauce slowly in a small saucepan. Be careful not to boil the sauce, or it may separate.

2 Chop the vegetarian bacon into ½-inch pieces.

3 Heat the oil in a sauté pan, add the garlic, and lightly brown. Add the mushrooms and continue to cook until tender.

4 Lightly steam the peas, making sure to retain their bright green color.

4 to 6 ounces vegetarian bacon, cooked according to package directions until dark brown and crispy, but not burned

1 teaspoon olive oil

2 teaspoons minced garlic

4 ounces shiitake or other mushrooms, stems removed, sliced

1 cup frozen baby peas or snow peas

8 ounce package fettuccine, linguini, or penne pasta

5 Cook the pasta according to package instructions until al dente, and drain.

6 Place the hot pasta, sauce, and all the other ingredients in a large pot, and toss together. Heat slowly and serve with a generous amount of soy Parmesan on the side. Delish!

Pad Thai-style Noodles
with Peanut Sauce

Yield: 3 to 4 servings

The peanut sauce provides a spicy, protein-rich change from traditional pasta recipes. The perfect vegetable to complement this pasta dish is the steamed Broccoli with Garlic, Tamari, and Coconut Sauce found on page 200.

8 ounces linguini pasta or rice noodles

2 zucchini

2 carrots

3 scallions, thinly sliced

1 cup frozen baby peas, thawed

1½ cups Spicy Thai Peanut Sauce, facing page

Per serving: Calories 433, Protein 10 g, Fat 9 g, Carbohydrate 75 g, Fiber 6 g, Calcium 52 mg, Sodium 237 mg

1 Cook the pasta according to the package instructions, and set aside.

2 While the pasta is cooking, cut the zucchini in half lengthwise, scoop out the seeds with a spoon, and slice ½ inch thick.

3 Peel the carrots and cut into 2 x ½-inch sticks.

4 Steam the vegetables 4 to 5 minutes, until just tender.

5 While the vegetables are steaming, prepare the peanut sauce in a large pot. If you prefer a thinner sauce, add more water.

6 Over medium heat, add the pasta and vegetables to the hot peanut sauce, toss, and serve when heated through.

Spicy Thai Peanut Sauce

Yield: 1⅓ cups

This sauce is excellent with vegetable kabobs, pasta, grains, or any Indonesian saté dish.

1 cup pure or distilled water

⅓ cup peanut butter, low-sodium if available

1 teaspoon minced garlic

2 teaspoons yellow miso

½ teaspoon Thai chili paste, or ⅛ teaspoon cayenne pepper

Per ⅓ cup: Calories 140, Protein 7 g, Fat 9 g, Carbohydrate 6 g, Fiber 2 g, Calcium 9 mg, Sodium 152 mg

1 Simmer half of the water and the remaining ingredients in a sauce pan.

2 Whip in the remaining water until the sauce reaches the desired consistency.

3 Adjust the seasonings to taste, and serve warm.

Penne Pasta
WITH GRILLED VEGETABLES AND PESTO SAUCE

Yield: 3 to 4 servings

3 portobello mushrooms

1 eggplant, stem removed, sliced
  ½ inch thick

2 tablespoons olive oil

1 tablespoon minced garlic

2 tablespoons chopped fresh basil or
  oregano

2 teaspoons Bragg Liquid Aminos

½ cup Pesto Sauce, page 64

8 ounces penne or other favorite
  pasta

¼ cup soy or rice Parmesan

Per serving: Calories 368, Protein 11 g,
Fat 25 g, Carbohydrate 28 g, Fiber 4 g,
Calcium 16 mg, Sodium 355 mg

1 Remove the stems from the mushrooms, and scrape out the gills underneath the caps.

2 Preheat the oven broiler to 550°F. Place the mushrooms, cap side up, and eggplant slices on a cookie sheet that has been lightly oiled with canola oil.

3 Make a marinade by placing the olive oil, garlic, basil or oregano, and Bragg in a blender and processing until smooth. Brush the marinade over the vegetables, place on the top oven rack, and broil for about 12 minutes until the eggplant is well-browned but not burned.

4 Allow the vegetables to cool slightly, then cut into 1½-inch squares.

5 Prepare the pesto sauce and set aside at room temperature.

6 Cook the pasta about 8 minutes, or until al dente, and drain.

7 In a large pan or bowl, toss the pasta with the pesto sauce, and fold in the vegetables. Reheat if necessary and serve with a generous garnish of soy Parmesan.

Sicilian-Style Orzo

Yield: 6 to 8 servings

Orzo is a rice–shaped pasta that cooks in 6 to 8 minutes. It is popular in Greek cuisine and a nice change from traditional pasta. This dish can also be served as a cold salad.

3 quarts distilled or pure water

1 pound whole wheat or tricolored orzo, or other small pasta

1 pound button mushrooms

3 tablespoons chopped fresh basil

1 tablespoon minced garlic

3 tablespoons extra-virgin olive oil

¼ teaspoon sea salt (optional)

Dash of cayenne pepper

4 ounces sun-dried tomatoes, softened in hot water and cut into ½-inch slices

¼ cup sliced black olives

¼ cup sliced green olives with pimientos

¼ cup capers (optional)

⅓ cup grated soy Parmesan

Per serving: Calories 189, Protein 7 g, Fat 8 g, Carbohydrate 21 g, Fiber 4 g, Calcium 20 mg, Sodium 303 mg

1 Bring the water to a rolling boil, add the pasta, and stir frequently. Cook 6 to 8 minutes, or until just tender. Steam the mushrooms and set aside.

2 Strain the pasta in a colander, rinse quickly with cool water, and strain. To reheat the orzo, pour scalding water over it and strain well.

3 Make a dressing by processing the basil, garlic, olive oil, salt, and cayenne in a blender until smooth.

4 In a large pan, heat the pasta with the dressing, and add the remaining ingredients.

5 Serve garnished with soy parmesan and a basil sprig.

Spinach Lasagne with Grilled Vegetables

Yield: 6 to 8 servings

If you enjoy using the barbecue grill, this low-fat lasagne will certainly appeal to you.

6 cups Marinara Sauce, page 61

1 eggplant

3 zucchini

3 summer squash

¼ cup extra-virgin olive oil

2 teaspoons minced garlic

1 small yellow or red bell pepper, quartered

1 tablespoon chopped fresh oregano

½ teaspoon sea salt (optional)

Dash of cayenne pepper

1 large red bell pepper

16 ounces spinach lasagne noodles or other lasagne noodles

8 ounces soy mozzarella, shredded

1 ounce soy Parmesan

Per serving: Calories 236, Protein 12 g, Fat 13 g, Carbohydrate 19 g, Fiber 5 g, Calcium 204 mg, Sodium 364 mg

1 Have the marinara sauce ready, and set aside.

2 Peel the eggplant and remove the stems from the zucchini and summer squash. Cut them lengthwise into long, ½-inch slices.

3 Preheat the grill on high.

4 In a blender, purée the olive oil, garlic, yellow or red bell pepper, oregano, salt, and cayenne. Brush a little additional oil over the sliced vegetables.

5 Place the vegetables on the grill until dark grill marks appear, then flip over and grill on the other side. If you would prefer using an oven, preheat the oven on the broil setting. Place the vegetables on a pan, brush with the oil mixture, and broil on the top rack for about 15 minutes until golden. Remove and cool the vegetables before proceeding.

6 Roast the red pepper until charred; remove the skin and slice ½ inch thick.

7 Preheat the oven to 400°F.

8 Line the bottom of a deep 10 x 13-inch, deep casserole dish with 2 cups of the marinara sauce to cover.

9 Layer enough uncooked noodles to cover the bottom of the pan, slightly overlapping, on the sauce.

10 Spread the grilled eggplant evenly over the noodles, and cover lightly with a little sauce.

11 Add another layer of the noodles over the eggplant, slightly overlapping, and cover with a little sauce.

12 Layer the zucchini evenly over the noodles, and cover with more noodles and sauce.

13 Place the grilled squash evenly over the noodles.

14 Sprinkle the soy mozzarella evenly over the squash, followed by the red pepper slices.

15 Cover the lasagne with plastic wrap, then with foil, and bake for 1 hour. Remove the lasagne.

16 Uncover the lasagne carefully and sprinkle the soy Parmesan over the top. Return to bake on the top oven rack until golden brown. Remove and allow to cool for about 10 minutes. This will allow the lasagne to "set up" and hold together well before cutting.

17 After cutting be sure to trim around the edges of the lasagne to loosen before serving. Reheat any remaining marinara sauce, and serve with the lasagne.

TOFU-VEGETABLE LASAGNE

Yield: 8 to 10 servings

The beauty of this recipe (besides the lower fat and calories) is the tremendous ease of assembly No more boiling your lasagne noodles, then hoping you have enough pieces to make one pan. Use the noodles right from the box. The kitchen staff here at the Regency is still rejoicing.

Tofu Filling

2 pounds firm tofu

2 tablespoons tahini

2 tablespoons yellow miso

4 ounces soy mozzarella, shredded

1 head broccoli, cut into florettes

1 cup julienned or thinly sliced carrots

½ pound fresh spinach, cleaned, stems removed, and sliced

1 zucchini and/or summer squash, quartered and sliced ½ inch thick

8 ounces mushrooms, sliced ½ inch thick

1 tablespoon coarsely chopped fresh basil

1½ quarts Marinara Sauce, page 61

16 ounces whole wheat or semolina lasagne noodles

8 ounces soy mozzarella, shredded

1 ounce soy or rice Parmesan

1 Press the excess water out of the tofu by wrapping it in a clean kitchen towel and placing a heavy pan or plate on top for 1 hour. Crumble or cut into cubes.

2 Blend the tofu, tahini, miso, and soy mozzarella in a food processor or in several batches in a blender until creamy.

3 Steam the broccoli and carrots for 3 minutes.

4 Combine all the filling ingredients, and set aside.

5 Preheat the oven to 400°F. You will need a 10 x 13-inch casserole dish or baking pan that is a minimum of 2½ inches deep.

6 Line the bottom of the pan with about 2 cups of the marinara sauce.

7   Layer about 5 of the uncooked noodles, slightly overlapping, over the sauce.

8   Spread a little more sauce evenly over the noodles.

9   Place half of the vegetable-tofu mix evenly over the noodles, packing firmly.

10   Place 1 more layer of lasagne noodles over the vegetable-tofu mix in same fashion as the first layer. If you need to break the noodles in order to fit them in the pan, do so, but remember to overlap them.

11   Pour a generous layer of marinara sauce evenly over the top layer of noodles.

12   Cover the pan with plastic wrap, then with foil, and bake for about 1 hour, 15 minutes.

13   Remove the lasagne, uncover carefully, and sprinkle the mozzarella followed by the soy Parmesan over the top. Return the lasagne to the top oven rack, and bake for about 10 minutes until the cheese is lightly browned. Remove and let cool for about 10 minutes. This will allow the lasagne to "set up" and hold together well for serving.

14   After cutting, be sure to trim around the edges of the lasagne to loosen before serving.

Per serving: Calories 426, Protein 34 g, Fat 17 g, Carbohydrate 39 g, Fiber 8 g, Calcium 472 mg, Sodium 502 mg

TOFU
Entrees

TOFU ENTREES

Introduction to Tofu

Tofu is made by curdling soymilk which is strained from a mixture of ground soybeans cooked in a large amount of water. Because it has a bland flavor and can absorb other flavors easily, tofu is ideal to use in vegetarian entrees. It's versatile enough to use in salads, dressings, and desserts, as well. If you freeze tofu, then thaw and press it dry, it takes on a chewy, meat-like texture, perfect for chili or burgers.

There are two types of tofu available: regular and silken. Both types come in extra-firm, firm, and soft densities. For tofu steaks and stir-fries, regular extra-firm or firm tofu is recommended. The custard-like texture of silken tofu makes it superb in dressings, desserts, and sauces.

There are approximately 120 calories in a 4-ounce serving of tofu and 6 grams of fat. However, less than ½ gram of the fat is saturated. Low-fat regular tofu will have even less fat. Tofu is also rich in protein, low in sodium, and a good source of iron, calcium, potassium, and vitamins B and E.

Most regular tofu is sold in vacuum-sealed tubs which are filled with water and have expiration dates stamped on them. Some people prefer to drain and press much of the water out of their tofu before cooking. To do this, drain the tofu and wrap in paper or cloth kitchen towels first. Unwrap and place the tofu in a colander with a bowl beneath. Place another bowl or pan on top of the tofu with another heavy object, like a melon or a book, inside to weigh it down. Press the tofu about 1 hour. At this point, you can cut the tofu into slices for grilling or cubes for a stir-fry, crumble or mash for lasagne, tofu salad, stuffed shells, or scrambled tofu, or blend to create creamy salad dressings. If you don't use all the tofu at once, cover with water and refrigerate. If you change the water every other day, the tofu should store well for 7 to 10 days.

Silken tofu only needs to be removed from its package and lightly wiped dry before proceeding as needed in salad dressings or hot or cold sauces. If it comes in an aseptic package, it does not need to be kept refrigerated until it is opened. There are low-fat varieties of silken tofu available as well.

If you are concerned about purchasing tofu which has been stored in open containers of water (as is often the case in Oriental groceries), make sure the environment is sanitary and the temperature of the tofu is maintained below 40 degrees. Then you can purchase with peace of mind. Otherwise, a safer bet is tofu that is sealed. You can find sealed tofu in the refrigerator section of most natural food stores and in the produce department of traditional supermarkets.

There are many tofu recipes throughout this book, from enchiladas to whipped cream. I am sure you will find many favorites and will become a tofu afficionado in a very short time!

Broccoli and Cheddar Quiche

Yield: 6 servings

This dish is a wonderful addition to a Sunday brunch or for dinner.

½ cup vegetable broth

1 Vidalia or yellow onion, diced

2 teaspoons minced garlic

½ head broccoli, cut into florettes, with a little sliced off the bottom of the stalks

1 whole wheat or rice pie crust

1 pound regular tofu, pressed dry

1 tablespoon Bragg Liquid Aminos

2 tablespoons lemon juice

1½ tablespoons stone-ground mustard

1 teaspoon curry powder (If you like it spicy.)

4 ounces soy cheddar or other variety cheese, shredded

Per serving: Calories 314, Protein 15 g, Fat 19 g, Carbohydrate 25 g, Fiber 5 g, Calcium 196 mg, Sodium 251 mg

1 Preheat the oven to 375°F.

2 Heat the vegetable broth in a saucepan with the onion, garlic, and broccoli. Let simmer for 6 to 8 minutes, or until the broccoli is just tender. Remove and let cool.

3 While the broccoli is cooking, prebake the pie shell for about 5 minutes, and set aside.

4 Break the tofu into pieces, and place the Bragg, lemon juice, mustard, and turmeric in a food processor with the tofu, and purée until creamy. If the mixture seems too thick and heavy, drizzle some of the liquid from the vegetables into the processor, and purée again.

5 In a large bowl, fold the cooked vegetables into the tofu mixture. Using a rubber spatula, fold this mixture evenly into the prebaked pie shell.

6 Cover the top of the mixture with the shredded soy cheddar. Place on the bottom rack of the oven, and bake for 35 to 40 minutes, or until a toothpick inserted into the center comes out clean and the middle of the quiche is firm to touch. Allow to cool 5 minutes before cutting.

"Eggless" Tofu Benedict

Yield: 4 servings

This egg– and butter–free dish is a nutritious and delicious breakfast or brunch entree.

1 pound extra-firm tofu

¼ cup fresh lemon juice

¼ cup extra-virgin olive oil

1 tablespoon Bragg Liquid Aminos

4 whole wheat English muffins, split, or 4 whole wheat bread slices, toasted

2 vine-ripe tomatoes, sliced ¼ inch thick

1½ cups Mock Béarnaise Sauce, page 63

Per serving: Calories 392, Protein 15 g, Fat 20 g, Carbohydrate 35 g, Fiber 4 g, Calcium 155 mg, Sodium 519 mg

1 Drain and press the water out of the tofu for 1 hour. Cut into 4 slices.

2 Make a marinade by placing the lemon juice, olive oil, and Bragg in a blender, and purée. Pour the marinade over the tofu slices.

3 Preheat the oven to broil. Allow the tofu to marinate while heating.

4 If the Béarnaise Sauce is not already warm, heat in a saucepan over low heat.

5 Remove the tofu slices from the marinade, place on a baking sheet, and broil on the top oven rack.

6 When the tofu has become somewhat golden in color, remove from the oven.

7 Place 2 English muffin halves or 1 piece of whole wheat bread on a plate.

8 Place 1 tofu slice over the toasted muffin or bread slice.

9 Place 2 to 3 tomato slices over the tofu slice.

10 Ladle about ¼ cup of the warm Béarnaise sauce over the tomatoes, and serve.

Eggplant Parmesan

Yield: 8 to 12 servings

This is much lower in fat than traditional eggplant Parmesan, and it's cholesterol-free. It's also easier to prepare when you oven-fry the eggplant.

Tofu Filling

1½ pounds firm tofu

2 tablespoons tahini

2 tablespoons yellow miso

1 tablespoon chopped fresh basil or parsley

4 ounces soy mozzarella, shredded

3 eggplants

2 cups whole wheat flour

½ cup Ener-G egg replacer

1½ cups water

4 cups whole wheat bread crumbs

2 tablespoons dried oregano

¼ cup canola oil

6 cups Marinara Sauce, page 61, or your favorite marinara sauce

8 ounces soy mozzarella, shredded

½ cup grated soy Parmesan

Per serving: Calories 467, Protein 32 g, Fat 22 g, Carbohydrate 40 g, Fiber 9 g, Calcium 390 mg, Sodium 626 mg

1 Drain and press the excess water out of the tofu for 1 hour. Combine in a food processor or blender with the remaining ingredients for the tofu filling; set aside.

2 Peel the eggplants and slice lengthwise into ½-inch-thick slices.

3 Place the whole wheat flour in a bowl. Combine the egg replacer and water in another bowl, and mix the whole wheat bread crumbs and oregano in a third bowl.

4 Dust the eggplant slices in the flour, then dip in the egg replacer mixture. Coat the slices with the bread crumb mixture, and place side by side on a baking sheet.

5 Lightly coat a sauté pan with canola oil, and pan-fry the eggplant over medium heat until golden brown and crispy on both sides. (To oven-fry, bake the eggplant slices in an oiled baking pan on the bottom rack of the oven until the bottoms are brown, about 20 minutes. Flip over and brown the other sides.)

6 Preheat the oven to 400°F.

7 Coat the bottom of an 9 x 13-inch baking pan with 1 cup of the marinara sauce.

8 Layer eggplant slices side by side over the sauce.

9 Completely cover the slices with the tofu mixture.

10 Spread 1 cup of the marinara sauce over the tofu mixture, and spread evenly.

11 Cover the sauce with more eggplant slices, cutting pieces if necessary to make them fit.

12 Spread 2 more cups of the marinara sauce over the eggplant.

13 Sprinkle with the soy mozzarella, then the Parmesan. Bake uncovered on the bottom oven rack for 35 to 40 minutes, or until slightly browned.

14 Remove the casserole from the oven, and let cool for 5 minutes before slicing. Serve with the remaining marinara sauce.

EGGPLANT ROLLATINI WITH MARINARA SAUCE

Yield: 6 servings

This low–calorie dish is delicious and easy to prepare.

2 tablespoons extra-virgin olive oil

1 tablespoon chopped fresh basil

1 teaspoon minced garlic

1 tablespoon Bragg Liquid Aminos

2 large eggplants, stems removed, bottoms trimmed, and cut lengthwise into ½-inch-thick slices (2 slices per person)

1 pound firm or extra-firm tofu, pressed dry

1 tablespoon white or yellow miso

1 tablespoon tahini

6 ounces soy mozzarella, shredded

1 cup chopped fresh spinach

2 cups marinara sauce

1 Preheat the oven on broil to 500°F.

2 Purée the olive oil, basil, garlic, and Bragg in a blender.

3 Place the eggplant on a lightly oiled baking sheet, and brush with the oil mixture.

Per serving: Calories 237, Protein 11 g, Fat 9 g, Carbohydrate 23 g, Fiber 6 g, Calcium 266 mg, Sodium 470 mg

4 Place the eggplant on the top oven rack, and broil for about 12 minutes, or until the eggplant is medium brown. Remove from the oven and let cool. Reduce the oven to 400°F.

5 Place the tofu, miso, tahini, and ⅔ cup of the shredded cheese in a food processor or blender, and purée until creamy. Spoon the tofu mixture into a small bowl, and fold in the spinach. Line a casserole dish generously with some of the marinara sauce.

6 To assemble, flip the eggplant slices onto a clean table with the cooked side down. Place one large spoonful of the tofu mixture in the center of the eggplant, and roll to close. Place the rolled eggplant slices side by side into the casserole, and cover with remaining marinara sauce.

7 Sprinkle the remaining soy cheese over the eggplant, place on the bottom oven rack, and bake for 18 to 20 minutes until the cheese is lightly browned. Serve with angel hair pasta or steamed vegetables.

Three Bean Enchiladas

Yield: 4 to 6 servings

If you are trying to get a "reluctant someone" to enjoy tofu for the first time, this could be the perfect dish. If time is a factor, you may substitute canned beans.

Bean Filling

⅓ cup pinto or kidney beans

⅓ cup black beans

1½ quarts distilled or pure water

2 bay leaves

1 tablespoon minced garlic

2 tablespoons ground cumin

⅛ teaspoon cayenne pepper

1 teaspoon sea salt (optional)

½ pound extra-firm tofu

1 zucchini

1 cup corn

4 ounces soy cheddar, shredded

4 ounces soy jalapeño Monterey Jack, shredded

Six 8-inch whole wheat tortillas

4 cups Enchilada Sauce, page 132

Per serving: Calories 358, Protein 14 g, Fat 4 g, Carbohydrate 64 g, Fiber 11 g, Calcium 114 mg, Sodium 218 mg

1 Sort the beans to remove any stones, and rinse. Soak in enough boiling water to cover for 1 to 2 hours.

2 In a large pot, bring the distilled water to a boil, strain the soaked beans, and add to the pot.

3 Add the bay leaves and remaining filling ingredients, and cook for 1 hour, or until the beans are tender.

4 Strain the beans and set aside until cool.

5 Drain the tofu and press out the excess liquid for about 1 hour. Cut into ¼-inch cubes, and set aside.

6 Slice the zucchini in half lengthwise, scoop out the seeds, and dice into ¼-inch cubes.

7 Preheat the oven to 400°F.

8 In a medium bowl, combine the beans, tofu, cubed zucchini, corn, 1 cup of the enchilada sauce, and half of the cheeses.

9 In a baking pan, ladle enough of the enchilada sauce to coat the bottom.

10 Place a tortilla on a plate. Spoon about ⅔ cup of the bean and tofu mix down the middle, fold over one side of the tortilla, and roll to close. Place in the pan on top of the sauce.

11 Continue until all the tortillas and bean mix have been used. Cover with the remaining sauce.

12 Sprinkle the remaining cheese over the enchiladas, and bake uncovered on the bottom oven rack for about 20 to 25 minutes until the cheese is melted but not brown.

13 Remove from the oven and serve hot with some Mexican salsa and guacamole. Garnish with black olives, jalapeño slices, and soy or rice sour cream, if you like.

Enchilada Sauce

Yield: about 1 quart

This spicy sauce can be served with any tortilla dish.

2 teaspoons extra-virgin olive oil

1 Vidalia or yellow onion, chopped

2 tablespoons minced garlic

1 red bell bell pepper, chopped

3 tablespoons whole wheat flour

3 tablespoons chile powder

One 8-ounce can tomato purée

1 cup vegetable broth or water

2 tablespoons cider vinegar

2 teaspoons ground cumin

1 tablespoon chopped fresh cilantro

Dash cayenne pepper

½ teaspoon sea salt (optional)

Per ¼ cup: Calories 84, Protein 2 g,
Fat 2 g, Carbohydrate 13 g, Fiber 3 g,
Calcium 21 mg, Sodium 26 mg

1 In a saucepan, heat the olive oil and lightly brown the onion and garlic.

2 Add the pepper and continue to cook about 3 minutes.

3 Lower the heat and slowly sprinkle in the flour and chile powder.

4 Whip in the remaining ingredients, adjusting spices to taste.

5 Cover and simmer for about 20 minutes, stirring occasionally. If any lumps remain, purée with a hand blender.

Grilled Tofu Steaks

Yield: 4 servings

The barbecue grill adds a delicious dimension to vegetarian cuisine, as this recipe will demonstrate. If you have no grill, pan–fry these with a little toasted sesame oil and drizzle the marinade over while browning.

1 pound extra-firm tofu

½ cup Oriental Vinaigrette, page 49, Hickory-Smoked Barbecue Sauce, page 59, or your favorite low-sodium marinade or sauce

Per serving: Calories 125, Protein 9 g, Fat 5 g, Carbohydrate 10 g, Fiber 1 g, Calcium 130 mg, Sodium 249 mg

1 Drain and press most of the water out of the tofu for 1 hour. Pat dry with a towel before slicing.

2 Cut the tofu into ½-inch-thick slices.

3 Pour enough marinade into a non-metallic pan to cover the bottom. Place the tofu slices in the pan, and top with more marinade.

4 Allow the tofu to marinate for 2 hours in the refrigerator.

5 Heat your grill at its hottest setting for about 5 minutes.

6 Rub the grill irons with a little canola oil, and cook the tofu slices on both sides until grill marks appear.

7 Serve with a little of the remaining marinade over the slices.

Scrambled Tofu

Yield: 3 to 4 servings

This is a our nutritious substitute for scrambled eggs. It's great for a fast breakfast or a protein-rich dish for any meal. Try other vegetables and herbs to add a little creativity to your dish! Scrambled tofu goes well on a whole wheat pita with sprouts and tomatoes or with Lyonnaise potatoes. Served cold, it can be a dairy-free egg salad. For a Tex-Mex version, garnish the scrambled tofu with Mexican salsa and guacamole or soy or rice sour cream and roll into a whole wheat or corn tortilla.

1 pound extra-firm tofu

1 small yellow onion

1 small red bell pepper

¼ cup vegetable broth or distilled water, or 1 teaspoon canola oil

1 cup sliced mushrooms (optional)

1 teaspoon minced garlic

1 to 2 teaspoons curry powder, or ½ teaspoon turmeric (if curry is too spicy for you)

1 tablespoon Bragg Liquid Aminos, or 1 teaspoon tamari or soy sauce

Per serving: Calories 122, Protein 10 g, Fat 5 g, Carbohydrate 7 g, Fiber 1 g, Calcium 149 mg, Sodium 200 mg

1 Drain and press most of the water out of the tofu, then crumble or mash with a potato masher.

2 Chop the onion and bell peppers. If using scallions, rinse and cut into ½-inch slices.

3 Heat a medium sauté pan over medium-high heat, and add either the vegetable broth, water, or canola oil.

4 Add the vegetables and steam or sauté until tender.

5 Add the tofu and remaining ingredients, and cook until hot, stirring occasionally with a wooden spoon or spatula. Drain any excess liquid and serve.

Tofu Meatballs

Yield: 4 to 6 servings

Even those guests who did not like tofu previously have found these tofu meatballs delicious. If you have a #20 ice cream scoop, making balls the right size is a snap.

2 pounds extra-firm tofu

1 yellow onion

1 red bell pepper

2 teaspoons olive oil, or ¼ cup vegetable broth

1 tablespoon minced garlic

1 tablespoon chopped fresh oregano

2 teaspoons chopped fresh thyme

⅛ teaspoon cayenne pepper

2 tablespoons tamari or soy sauce

Per serving: Calories 172, Protein 14 g, Fat 9 g, Carbohydrate 7 g, Fiber 1 g, Calcium 201 mg, Sodium 416 mg

1 Drain and press the excess water out of the tofu for 1 hour.

2 Dice the onion and bell pepper into ½-inch cubes.

3 In a medium sauté pan, heat the oil or water and sauté or steam the vegetables until golden brown or tender.

4 In a mixing bowl, mash or crumble the tofu into small pieces.

5 Add the vegetables and remaining ingredients, and mix thoroughly.

6 Preheat the oven to 425°F.

7 Lightly oil a baking sheet with canola oil. Scoop up about ¼ cup of the tofu mixture, and tightly mold into a ball with your hands. Place on the baking sheet, and continue with the remaining mix.

8 Bake the tofu balls for 45 minutes, or until well browned. Serve with your favorite pasta and sauce or garlic-mashed potatoes and gravy.

THANKSGIVING TURKEY-STYLE TOFU LOAF

Yield: 3 to 4 servings

Using frozen tofu gives this dish its amazing meat–like texture. The nutritional yeast breading is rich in protein and all of the essential amino acids.

1 pound extra-firm tofu

2 quarts boiling water

2 tablespoons low-sodium tamari or soy sauce

¼ cup water

½ cup nutritional yeast

1 tablespoon garlic powder

1 teaspoon canola oil

Per serving: Calories 173, Protein 17 g, Fat 7 g, Carbohydrate 10 g, Fiber 1 g, Calcium 176 mg, Sodium 375 mg

1 Drain and press the excess water out of the tofu, then cover with plastic wrap and freeze for at least 24 hours.

2 Preheat the oven to 375°F.

3 Remove the tofu from the freezer, and place in the boiling water for 5 minutes.

4 Place the tofu in a strainer, and press again to drain.

5 Dip the tofu in the tamari quickly, rotating it from side to side to coat evenly. (The longer you let the tofu sit in the tamari, the saltier it will become.)

6 Combine the nutritional yeast and garlic powder in a shallow bowl, and roll the tofu in the mix to coat evenly.

7 Lightly oil a baking pan with the canola oil, and bake the tofu for 45 minutes, or until brown.

8 Remove from the oven, slice, and serve hot or cold.

WILD MUSHROOM DRESSING

Yield: 4 to 6 servings

This hearty dressing is a holiday favorite. Serve it with
Turkey–Style Tofu Loaf, page 136, and Savory Gravy, page 65.

3 portobello mushrooms, or 8 ounces shiitake mushrooms

1 teaspoon canola oil

1 large Vidalia or yellow onion, chopped

1 teaspoon minced garlic

8 slices whole wheat bread, cut into 1-inch cubes

2 teaspoons sage

1 cup Savory Gravy, page 65, plus all of the vegetables from the gravy

Per serving: Calories 138, Protein 6 g, Fat 3 g, Carbohydrate 23 g, Fiber 6 g, Calcium 13 mg, Sodium 201 mg

1. Preheat the oven to 375°F.

2. Scoop out the gills on the undersides of the portobello mushrooms, or remove the stems from the shiitake mushrooms and slice.

3. Heat the oil in a sauté pan, and sauté the onions and garlic until lightly brown.

4. Add the mushrooms, cover, and cook until tender.

5. Strain most of the liquid off the mushrooms, and toss with the bread cubes and sage.

6. Fold in some of the Savory Gravy and all of the vegetables from the gravy until the bread cubes are moist.

7. Place the dressing in a 10 x 13-inch casserole, and bake for 30 to 40 minutes until the top is crispy.

Tofu Eggplant Torte

Yield: 6 to 8 servings

This delicious lasagne–style dish was an immediate hit at the spa.

2 pounds extra-firm tofu, pressed dry

2 tablespoons low-sodium tamari

½ cup water

1 tablespoon chopped fresh oregano

2 teaspoons minced garlic

1 large eggplant, stem removed and sliced lengthwise into ¾-inch-thick slices

2 tablespoons olive oil

1 teaspoon minced garlic

1 Preheat the oven to 400°F. Slice each pound of tofu into 4 slices for steaks.

2 Place the tofu steaks on a sheet pan.

3 Purée the tamari, water, oregano, and 2 teaspoons garlic in a blender. Pour this marinade over the tofu steaks, and bake for 35 to 40 minutes, or until the marinade has evaporated from the pan. Remove from the oven and allow the tofu to cool.

4 Set the oven to broil at 550°F. Place the eggplant slices on a lightly oiled cookie sheet.

5 Purée the olive oil, 1 teaspoon garlic, and half of the basil in a blender, and place in a small bowl.

6 Using a pastry brush, brush the top side of the eggplant lightly with the marinade, and place on the top oven rack. Broil for about 12 minutes, or until the eggplant is medium brown in color. Remove and allow to cool. Return the oven setting to 400°F.

7 While the tofu and eggplant are roasting, sauté the onion, mushrooms, and thyme in the broth until tender.

8 To assemble, place 1 cup of the marinara sauce in an 8-inch square casserole. Place 4 pieces of the tofu steaks side by side in the bottom of the casserole. It is alright to cut the tofu to fit into the pan correctly.

2 tablespoons chopped fresh basil

3 portobello mushrooms, stems removed, gills scraped out, and cut into ½-inch slices

1 Vidalia or yellow onion, peeled, cut in half, and cut into ¼-inch-slices

1 teaspoon chopped fresh thyme

¼ cup vegetable broth or nonalcoholic white wine

3 cups marinara sauce

Half 10-ounce package fresh spinach, stems removed and torn into small pieces

⅔ cup sun-dried tomatoes, softened in warm water and cut into ½-inch slices

8 ounces soy mozzarella, garlic and herb, or other soy cheese, shredded

Per serving: Calories 386, Protein 32 g, Fat 21 g, Carbohydrate 24 g, Fiber 8 g, Calcium 490 mg, Sodium 716 mg

9 Place the grilled eggplant over the tofu, and sprinkle the spinach leaves over the eggplant.

10 Layer the mushroom mixture over the spinach, and sprinkle ¼ of the soy cheese over the mushrooms.

11 Place the remaining tofu steaks over the vegetables, and spread enough of the marinara to cover the tofu completely.

12 Sprinkle the remaining cheese over the tofu, and garnish with the rest of the chopped basil.

13 Bake on the bottom rack of the oven for about 25 minutes, or until the cheese is lightly browned. Remove the casserole from the oven, and allow to rest for about 5 minutes before cutting. Serve with the remaining marinara sauce and your favorite whole grain bread or vegetables.

Tofu Terrine
WITH SUN-DRIED TOMATOES AND PESTO SAUCE

Yield: 8 to 10 servings

I have always wanted to recreate one of my favorite cheeses (goat cheese) using tofu as the replacement. This casserole–style dish has made a believer out of many of our guests. This dish can be served sliced on whole grain crackers or bread, over a bed of assorted greens as an entree–type salad, or as is. It is delicious either way.

2 pounds firm or extra-firm regular tofu, pressed dry

2 tablespoons yellow or white miso

2 tablespoons tahini

2 ounces soy mozzarella, shredded

⅔ cup sun-dried tomatoes, softened in warm water and thinly sliced

½ cup Pesto Sauce, page 64

Per serving: Calories 184, Protein 11 g, Fat 13 g, Carbohydrate 6 g, Fiber 1 g, Calcium 165 mg, Sodium 256 mg

1 Preheat the oven to 375°F.

2 Line a casserole dish of your choice with aluminum foil. I have used round pie pans or rectangular loaf pans for this dish. There is no rule of thumb for which type of pan to use. Just be sure you have enough tofu filling to make 2 layers in the pan.

3 Purée the tofu, miso, tahini, and soy cheese in a food processor or blender until creamy. Scrape down the sides of the blender with a spatula to eliminate all lumps.

4 Spread half of the tofu mixture evenly in the bottom of the casserole.

5 Place an even layer of the sun-dried tomatoes across the tofu mixture.

6 Spread the pesto sauce evenly over the sun-dried tomatoes.

7 Carefully spread the remaining tofu mixture evenly over the pesto and tomatoes.

8 Cover the pan with foil, and place it inside of another pan. Add some water to the bottom pan to use as a water bath while baking. This prevents burning the bottom of the casserole.

9 Bake for 45 to 50 minutes on the bottom oven rack. Remove, uncover, and chill in the freezer for about 1 hour. Once cooled, peel back the foil from the sides of the casserole, using a paring knife to trim the tofu from the foil if necessary.

10 Invert the casserole onto a cutting board or tray for serving. To do this, place the tray or cutting board over the casserole, and flip it over onto the board. Tap the bottom of the inverted casserole with the handle of a knife to loosen it. Remove the dish and peel back the foil. Place it in the refrigerator for further cooling, then slice as needed.

RICE
Entrees

RICE

History and Cooking Techniques

We recommend using brown rice in the recipes in this book because of its superior nutritional value. Brown rice is produced after the first milling of whole rice where the inedible husk is removed. At this point, the rice has retained its nutrients, fiber-dense bran, and germ. Brown rice is available in long, medium, and short grain. The short grain cooks up somewhat stickier and more moist and is best used in puddings, sushi, and casseroles. The longer grains are predominantly used in entrees and side dishes. We recommend using brown rice within one month of purchase if stored at room temperature. Otherwise, it is best to refrigerate the rice, because the germ is prone to becoming rancid.

Further milling of the rice produces white or polished rice. Polishing removes the bran, germ, fiber, and B vitamins! Enriched white rice, like enriched bread, has had some of the nutrients added back, but not the fiber or trace elements.

Converted rice goes back to World War II when husked rice was parboiled and dried before milling. In this process, vitamins and minerals in the bran layer are forced into the rice kernel, creating a more nutritious product.

Long grain rice (rice that is four times longer than it is wide) includes basmati from India, jasmine from Thailand, Texmati (a basmati grown in Texas), and popcorn and pecan rice from Louisiana, known for its nutty fragrance. Other long grain varieties include red rice, Thai black rice, Wehani (a basmati and red bran rice), and black Japonica (mahogany and black rice).

The art of cooking rice varies among countries and cuisines. A simple rule of thumb is to always rinse the rice in a strainer first. If serving the rice plain, 2 cups of boiling water to 1 cup of dry rice is a good ratio. If you are sautéing onions, garlic, or other vegetables before adding the rice and water, use a little less than 2 cups of water. When the water comes to the second boil after the rice has been added, cover and simmer for about 20 minutes. Lower the heat to warm, and allow another 15 minutes for the remaining liquid to evaporate. Some of us like our rice a little firmer than others, so if the rice has come to the tenderness you prefer and liquid is still present, you may strain the rice quickly and return it to the pot. Cover and let rest for about 10 minutes.

I hope this information will give you the confidence to make the correct choices when purchasing and cooking rice.

FLORENTINE RICE

Yield: 4 to 6 servings

This entree is also delicious served chilled for a cold lunch or buffet salad.

⅓ cup pine nuts

1 teaspoon extra-virgin olive oil

1 Vidalia onion, chopped

2 teaspoons minced garlic

8 ounces mushrooms, cut in half

1 red, yellow, or orange bell pepper, chopped (If time allows, roast and peel first before chopping.)

½ cup julienned sun-dried tomatoes

3½ cups scalding hot distilled or pure water

2 cups brown basmati, jasmine, or other brown rice

1 bay leaf

1 teaspoon sea salt (optional)

⅛ teaspoon cayenne pepper

4 ounces fresh spinach, cleaned, stems removed, and cut in half (2½ to 3 cups)

Per serving: Calories 263, Protein 7 g, Fat 6 g, Carbohydrate 44 g, Fiber 5 g, Calcium 53 mg, Sodium 30 mg

1 Roast the pine nuts at 400°F in a baking pan in the oven until lightly brown.

2 In a large pot, heat the oil and sauté the onions and garlic until lightly browned. Add the mushrooms and simmer.

3 Add remaining ingredients, except the spinach; cover and simmer for 20 minutes.

4 When about ¾ of the liquid is gone, fold in the spinach, lower the heat to warm, and cover.

5 Serve when the rice is tender or the water has evaporated. If the rice is tender to your liking before the water is completely gone, place the rice in a strainer to remove the excess water, then return to the pot and cover until ready to serve.

SOUTHWESTERN RICE

This dish is great as a hot entree or as a chilled salad! I like to melt some shredded soy cheese over this dish for even more flavor and nutrition.

3½ cups distilled or pure water

1 bay leaf

1 teaspoon saffron threads or turmeric

2 tablespoons chili powder

2 cups brown basmati rice

½ teaspoon sea salt (optional)

2 cups cooked, drained black beans

2 cups yellow corn, cut from the cob or frozen corn, steamed

1 tablespoon finely chopped cilantro

1½ cups Mexican Salsa, page 62

Per serving: Calories 197, Protein 6 g, Fat 0 g, Carbohydrate 42 g, Fiber 7 g, Calcium 20 mg, Sodium 519 mg

1 Bring the water to a boil, and add the bay leaf, saffron or turmeric, chili powder, and rice.

2 Cover and cook for 25 minutes, or until most of the liquid has evaporated.

3 Turn off the heat, cover, and let sit until all the liquid has been absorbed.

4 Heat the black beans, corn, cilantro, and salsa in a medium saucepan. Fold into the rice and serve hot.

RED BEANS AND RICE

Yield: 6 to 8 servings

When rice and beans are combined, they become a complete protein with all of the essential amino acids. You may substitute any of your favorite beans or lentils for the red beans in this recipe. (If time is a factor you may substitute canned beans, but be sure to check the sodium content before purchasing.)

1 pound red beans

2½ quarts distilled water

2 bay leaves

2 tablespoons minced garlic

1 Vidalia or yellow onion, chopped

1 red bell pepper, chopped

1 yellow or orange bell pepper, chopped

1½ tablespoons ground cumin

Dash of cayenne pepper

2 tablespoons Bragg Liquid Aminos

1 Soak the beans in enough scalding water to cover for 1 to 2 hours.

2 In a large pot, bring the 2½ quarts distilled water to a boil. Strain the beans and add to the pot.

3 Add the 2 bay leaves and garlic, and simmer for 1 hour.

4 Add the onion, peppers, cumin, cayenne, and liquid aminos, and cook for 1 hour, or until the beans are tender.

5 Adjust the seasonings to taste, and set aside.

6 In another large pot, bring the 3½ cups water to a boil, and add the rice and the remaining bay leaf.

3½ cups distilled or pure water

2 cups brown basmati, jasmine, or
  other brown rice

1 bay leaf

Per serving: Calories 220, Protein 8 g,
Fat 0 g, Carbohydrate 45 g, Fiber 5 g,
Calcium 50 mg, Sodium 193 mg

7 Cover and cook for about 25
  minutes, or until most of the liquid is gone.

8 Lower the heat to simmer and
  keep covered until the rice is
  tender or the water has been
  absorbed. If the rice is tender to
  your liking before the water is
  completely gone, place the rice in
  a strainer to remove the excess
  water, then return to the pot and
  cover.

9 Fold the beans into the rice,
  adding a little of the bean broth
  until the consistency of rice to
  beans is to your liking.

Vegetable Sushi Rolls

Yield: 3 to 4 rolls (5 to 6 pieces per roll)

This versatile dish can be served as an entree, appetizer, hors d'oeuvre, or snack. we use our fabulous Oriental Vinaigrette on page 49 as a dipping sauce.

3¾ cups pure or distilled water

1 teaspoon sea salt (optional)

2 cups short grain brown rice, preferably basmati

1 bunch scallions, cut in ¼-inch slices

2 tablespoons umeboshi plum paste (optional—use less if you're watching your sodium intake)

2 carrots

1 cucumber

1 red bell pepper

1 ripe avocado

1 pint alfalfa sprouts

4 sushi nori sheets

1 bamboo sushi rolling mat

Per serving: Calories 77, Protein 1 g, Fat 1 g, Carbohydrate 14 g, Fiber 2 g, Calcium 16 mg, Sodium 124 mg

1 Bring the water and salt to a boil. Place the rice in a strainer, and rinse with cool water. Add the rice to the pot, cover, and boil gently for 20 to 25 minutes. When most of the water has been absorbed, lower the heat and continue to cook until the water has been absorbed.

2 Remove the rice from the pot, place in a large bowl, and fold in the plum paste and sliced scallions. Allow the rice to cool to room temperature.

3 Hand-grate or shred the carrots in a food processor.

4 Peel the cucumber, cut in half lengthwise, and remove the seeds with a spoon. Cut into long strips ½ inch thick.

5 Cut the bell pepper in half, remove the seeds, and julienne.

6 Cut the avocado in half, remove the pit and shell, and cut into ½-inch slices.

7 To assemble, place all the cut vegetables and rice at the back of a clean counter top. Place a bowl of cool water to the side for dipping your fingers when they get starchy and to seal the ends of the nori rolls later in the process.

8 Place the sushi mat in front of you horizontally, then place 1 sushi nori sheet, shiny side down, on the mat. Be sure the nori sheets are aligned with the horizontal rows of the bamboo mat.

9 Spoon the rice mixture about ½ inch thick evenly over the nori sheet, leaving about 1 inch on the nori sheet closest to you and 2 inches furthest from you without rice. Refer to the sushi rolling diagram at right.

10 Along the center of the rice, spread ¼ of the carrots and vegetables evenly, allowing the vegetables to extend slightly past the end of the nori sheets.

11 To roll, lift up the edge of the mat closest to you and roll away from you about one-quarter of a turn, rolling the mat, nori sheet, and rice over the filling. Press down a little to help the rice hold together, and press the vegetables into the rice slightly with your fingers as you continue to roll the mat and nori around the rice. Since the nori itself is somewhat fragile, the mat helps protect it as you form the roll.

12 Once the roll has been formed, dip your fingers in the water and seal the nori sheet along the side where it meets to seal. Allow to dry. (Repeat steps 7 through 12 with the remaining ingredients.)

13 Use a long, sharp knife to trim the ends of the roll. Either cut the roll into 1-inch slices, or vary from the traditional presentation by making a diagonal cut on one side and a straight cut on the other side to give the rolls different heights and angles. Serve with wasabi, pickled ginger, and/or low-sodium soy sauce or tamari.

ETHNIC
and
Miscellaneous
Entrees

BLACK BEAN AND CORN QUESADILLAS

Yield: 6 servings

This Mexican version of a grilled cheese sandwich can be made in just minutes. Serve with Mexican salsa, guacamole, and/or rice sour cream. At home when time is a factor, we like to eliminate the vegetables and make a plain cheese quesadilla for an easy meal after a long day.

One 16-ounce can black beans, drained

One 16-ounce can corn, drained

3 scallions, thinly sliced

⅔ cup Mexican Salsa, page 62

12 ounces soy cheddar

8 ounces soy jalapeño Monterey Jack

6 whole wheat tortillas or chapatis (Chapatis will result in a softer texture.)

Per serving: Calories 481, Protein 32 g, Fat 14 g, Carbohydrate 60 g, Fiber 11 g, Calcium 475 mg, Sodium 779 mg

1 In a bowl, combine the beans, corn, scallions, and salsa. Shred the cheeses.

2 Place the tortillas on a flat surface, and sprinkle the cheese evenly over half of each tortilla.

3 Spread equal amounts of the bean mixture evenly over the cheese, sprinkle with more cheese, and fold the empty side over to make a half-moon shape.

4 Heat a sauté pan over medium-high heat, and brush lightly with canola oil. Place a tortilla in the pan, and cook until lightly browned on one side; repeat quickly on the other side.

5 When the cheese has melted but is not too runny, remove and place on a cutting board.

6 Cook the remaining filled tortillas. Allow to cool slightly before cutting into pie-shaped wedges. Serve warm.

Chicken Seitan Stroganoff

The debut of this item last summer was just mouth-watering. The rice sour cream is the secret.

1 teaspoon olive oil, or ⅓ cup vegetable broth

1 Vidalia or yellow onion, diced

1 tablespoon minced garlic

1 pound button mushrooms, sliced

4 ounces shiitake mushrooms, stems removed, sliced

1 cup vegetable broth

¼ cup tomato purée

1 tablespoon Bragg Liquid Aminos

1 teaspoon chopped fresh thyme

Dash of cayenne pepper

2 tablespoons arrowroot powder dissolved in ⅓ cup cool water

½ cup rice sour cream

One 8-ounce package chicken-style seitan, drained and cut into ¼-inch-thick slices (Reserve the liquid.)

¼ cup garlic, chives, or scallion tops, cut into ¼-inch slices

Per serving: Calories 252, Protein 27 g, Fat 5 g, Carbohydrate 23 g, Fiber 3 g, Calcium 19 mg, Sodium 231 mg

1 Heat the olive oil or vegetable broth, and sauté the onion until lightly browned. Add the garlic and mushrooms, and continue to cook until the mushrooms are tender.

2 Add the vegetable broth, tomato purée, Bragg, thyme, and cayenne, and cook for about 5 minutes.

3 Whip in the arrowroot and water mixture, and continue to cook until thickened. Fold in the rice sour cream, adjust the seasonings to taste, and simmer. If a thicker sauce is desired, add more arrowroot mixture.

4 Add the chicken seitan and simmer until hot; adjust the spices as necessary.

5 Serve as is or over brown rice pilaf or pasta, and garnish with chives.

Chicken-style Seitan Marsala

Yield: 4 servings

Seitan, also called "wheat meat," is made from wheat gluten. It can be used to replace meat in almost any recipe.

1 teaspoon olive or canola oil

1 yellow onion, chopped

1 tablespoon minced garlic

8 ounces button or shiitake mushrooms, cut into ½-inch slices

8 ounces chicken-style seitan, sliced into strips

⅔ cup marsala or sweet red wine

1 teaspoon chopped fresh thyme

1 teaspoon chopped fresh marjoram or Italian parsley

¼ cup arrowroot

¼ cup pure or distilled water

Per serving: Calories 169, Protein 20 g, Fat 1 g, Carbohydrate 18 g, Fiber 1 g, Calcium 16 mg, Sodium 6 mg

1 Heat the oil in a sauté pan, add the onion and garlic, and sauté for 5 minutes.

2 Add the mushrooms and simmer for 5 minutes.

3 Add the seitan and sauté until heated.

4 Add the wine and herbs, and bring to a simmer.

5 Dissolve the arrowroot in the water, and whip into the mushroom sauce until thickened.

6 Adjust the spices as desired, and serve over warm pasta, brown rice, or quinoa.

CHINESE FRIED RICE

Yield: 4 servings

This recipe is actually prepared without frying the rice. No one will ever know the difference. This rice goes well with grilled tofu steaks, page 133, or stir–fried asparagus and bok choy, page 198. If you want an authentic chopped egg look to your fried rice, try folding in some scrambled tofu, page 134. If you have a rice cooker, you can use it in this recipe.

1 quart pure or distilled water

¼ cup low-sodium tamari or soy sauce

2 cups brown basmati rice, rinsed with cool water and strained

3 scallions, sliced

1½ cups frozen peas, thawed

2 cups bean sprouts

1 teaspoon toasted sesame oil

Per serving: Calories 289, Protein 10 g, Fat 2 g, Carbohydrate 58 g, Fiber 7 g, Calcium 55 mg, Sodium 610 mg

1 Bring the water and tamari to a boil in a medium pot. Sprinkle in the rice and cover. Simmer over medium heat, being careful not to have the heat up so high that the rice bubbles over the side of the pot. Do not stir the rice while it is cooking. Keep the rice covered the entire time, as well. These precautions will reduce the starchiness of the rice. After about 20 minutes, take a peak. When you begin to see air pockets on the top of the rice, it is almost finished. Lower the heat to low, and keep covered for about 15 minutes.

2 In a wok or large sauté pan, heat the sesame oil and toss in the scallions. Fold in the rice and all the other ingredients until everything is hot. Adjust the seasonings to taste.

CRISPY TEMPEH

Yield: 4 servings

If you are not familiar with tempeh, it is a fermented soybean cake with a light flavor similar to mushrooms. You can also find tempeh made with a combination of soybeans and grains, or a combination of grains. Tempeh is extremely high in protein. Serve this either with pita bread and your favorite salad items, crumbled on a tossed salad or baked potato, or add to a pasta primavera salad to give it that crispy texture.

8-ounces tempeh

⅓ cup Bragg Liquid Aminos

⅓ cup distilled water

1 teaspoon minced garlic

½ teaspoon minced fresh ginger

½ teaspoon liquid hickory smoke (optional—for a more "bacon-like" flavor)

Per serving: Calories 118, Protein 11 g, Fat 4 g, Carbohydrate 10 g, Fiber 3 g, Calcium 55 mg, Sodium 221 mg

1 Preheat the oven to 400°F.

2 Slice the tempeh ⅛ inch thick.

3 In a blender, combine the Bragg, water, garlic, ginger, and liquid hickory smoke.

4 Pour the mixture into a non-metallic bowl. Add the sliced tempeh to the mixture, and marinate for about 20 minutes.

5 Drain the tempeh into a colander.

6 Lightly oil a baking sheet with canola oil.

7 Place the tempeh on the baking sheet, and bake for about 30 minutes, until brown on one side.

8 Remove from the oven, flip the tempeh with a spatula, and return to the oven. Bake about 15 minutes more, or until brown and crispy.

FALAFEL PATTIES

Makes 8 to 10 patties

In Israel, falafel are a snack food as common as popcorn or an ice cream are here. Falafel are fried chick-pea patties. Over time the term has come to mean both the pita sandwich and the patty. We oven-fry the patties in this recipe, which makes them lower in fat than traditional fried falafel. Serve in a whole wheat pita with shredded lettuce and basil tahini or mustard tahini dressing.

2 cups cooked chick-peas

1 small Vidalia or yellow onion, chopped

1 tablespoon minced garlic

1 teaspoon toasted sesame oil

⅓ cup soy yogurt or soy sour cream

2 tablespoons stone-ground mustard

2½ cups whole wheat bread crumbs

2 tablespoons chopped fresh parsley

1 tablespoon Bragg Liquid Aminos

½ teaspoon ground cumin

¼ teaspoon paprika

Dash of cayenne pepper

Per serving: Calories 139, Protein 6 g, Fat 2 g, Carbohydrate 22 g, Fiber 3 g, Calcium 40 mg, Sodium 275 mg

1 Drain the beans and reserve the liquid.

2 In a sauté pan, brown the onions and garlic lightly in the sesame oil.

3 Place all the ingredients, except 2 cups of the bread crumbs, in a food processor or in batches in a blender, and chop coarsely. Do not purée the beans totally; allow for that coarser texture. If the mixture is too dry, add some of the reserved liquid.

4 Refrigerate the mix for 20 to 30 minutes, and preheat the oven to 425°F.

5 When the mix has cooled, form into ½-inch-thick patties. The patty can be 2 inches wide or can be made burger sized to fit the pita bread when cut in half. Coat the patties with the reserved bread crumbs.

6 Place the patties on a baking sheet oiled with canola oil, and bake until crispy on the bottom. Remove from the oven, flip the patties, and bake 15 minutes more until crispy on both sides.

Enchilada Pie

Yield: 6 to 8 servings

This delicious combination of corn tortillas, beans, vegetables, and soy cheese is loved by all of our guests. It also freezes very well if you are cooking for more than one meal. Garnish this with guacamole and salsa.

1 cup cooked black beans, drained

1 cup cooked pinto or kidney beans, drained

1 cup corn kernels

1 cup Mexican-Style Salsa, page 62, or your favorite brand

4 ounces soy cheddar, shredded

4 ounces soy jalapeño Monterey Jack, shredded

3 cups Enchilada Sauce, page 132

12 yellow corn tortillas

⅓ cup sliced black olives

1 jalapeño pepper, sliced (optional) (for note on handling hot peppers, see page 12)

1 Preheat the oven to 400°F.

2 In a large bowl, mix together the beans, corn, salsa, and half of each type of cheese.

3 Line an 8 x 8-inch casserole dish with 1 cup of enchilada sauce.

(continued on page 161)

Clockwise from top: Grilled Tofu Steaks, p. 133, Scrambled Tofu, p. 134, and Tofu Meatballs, p. 135.

4 Place the tortillas along the bottom of the casserole dish, slightly overlapping them. Spread half of the bean mixture over the tortillas.

5 Cover the beans with a layer of the tortillas, and coat with ½ cup of the enchilada sauce.

6 Place the remaining bean mixture over the tortillas, and cover with a final layer of tortillas. There may be few tortillas leftover that can be used later for Mexican Tortilla Soup, page 82-83, or homemade nacho chips.

7 Cover the tortillas with the remaining enchilada sauce. Sprinkle the remaining cheese over the sauce, garnish with the olive and jalapeño slices, and bake on the bottom oven rack for about 25 to 30 minutes until hot and bubbly. Remove the casserole before the cheese has browned for better appearance and texture.

Per serving: Calories 475, Protein 22 g, Fat 9 g, Carbohydrate 78 g, Fiber 15 g, Calcium 242 mg, Sodium 365 mg

Vegetable quesadillas, made from Grilled Vegetables, p. 203, roasted red peppers, p. 205, and fat–free soy cheeses. (See also Black Bean and Corn Quesadillas, p. 154.)

Grilled Vegetable Burritos

Yield: 6 servings

This is one of our most requested entrees. You may want to prepare extras so you'll have plenty for second helpings. For a more traditional burrito, replace the grilled vegetables with meatless chili and/or refried beans. Serve with guacamole, Mexican salsa, refried beans, or soy sour cream.

2 portobello mushrooms

1 large zucchini

1 large yellow squash

2 tablespoons extra-virgin olive oil

1 teaspoon minced garlic

1 teaspoon oregano leaves

Dash of cayenne pepper

1 large red bell pepper

4 ounces soy jalapeño Monterey Jack

4 ounces soy cheddar

Six 8-inch or larger whole wheat
 flour tortillas

*Per serving: Calories 226, Protein 12 g,
Fat 11 g, Carbohydrate 26 g, Fiber 3 g,
Calcium 196 mg, Sodium 414 mg*

1 Rinse and remove the stems from the portobello mushrooms. Scrape off the gills from the undersides of the mushrooms with a spoon. Slice the zucchini and yellow squash diagonally ½ inch thick.

2 Preheat your barbecue grill to high and your oven to 400°F.

3 Blend the olive oil, garlic, and oregano, and brush onto the vegetables.

4 Grill the vegetables on both sides until grill marks occur, and set aside. If you prefer to use your oven instead of the grill, turn the oven to broil and grill the vegetables on the top oven rack in an oiled baking pan for 12 to 15 minutes until slightly golden.

5 Roast the bell pepper skin side down on the grill or under the oven broiler with the skin side up until most of the skin is black. Place in a plastic bag to steam. When cooled, remove the pepper and peel the skin. Cut into 1-inch strips.

6 Slice the mushrooms ½ inch thick. Shred the cheeses and set aside.

7 Place a tortilla on a flat surface, and sprinkle evenly with the cheese.

8 Place 2 slices of zucchini, squash, and mushrooms end to end along the center of the tortilla, leaving about 1 inch of tortilla empty at the bottom.

9 Add slices of red pepper end to end over the vegetables.

10 Fold the bottom of the tortilla over the end of the vegetable strips.

11 Roll one side of the tortilla over the vegetables, keeping the bottom tucked in, and continue to roll rather tightly until closed. Repeat with the remaining tortillas and filling.

12 Place the burritos in a 10 x 13-inch casserole lined with foil to prevent them from sticking. Cover with foil and bake at 400°F for 15 minutes, or until the cheese is melted.

Grilled Vegetable Paella

Yield: 6 to 8 servings

The first time I had paella (pi—ay–ya) was 1982 in Tampa, Florida. I thought I had gone to seafood heaven. You never forget culinary moments like that. Traditional paella evolves around yellow rice, fresh local fish, and a variety of shellfish such as lobster, shrimp, scallops, clams, and mussels. In addition, chicken breast and some variety of sausage, such as chorizo, are added.

1 zucchini

1 small eggplant

3 portobello mushrooms

2 red bell peppers

1 quart distilled or pure water

2 tablespoons yellow or white miso

1 teaspoon turmeric, or 1 tablespoon saffron

2 cups basmati brown rice

1 bay leaf

⅓ cup olive oil

1 tablespoon chopped fresh basil, cilantro, or oregano

2 teaspoons minced garlic

1 tablespoon Bragg Liquid Aminos

Dash of cayenne pepper

4 vegetarian Italian sausage links

1½ ounces vegetarian pepperoni slices (about 20 slices)

1½ cup frozen baby peas, thawed and drained

1 Remove the ends of the zucchini and eggplant. Cut the zucchini lengthwise and the eggplant into circles, all ¾ inch thick. Remove the stems from the portobellos and scrape away the gills from the undersides of the caps with a spoon. Remove the seeds from the peppers, and cut into quarters.

2 Preheat the oven broiler to 550°F. Combine the water, miso, and turmeric in a large pot, and bring to a boil, Add the rice and bay leaf, cover, and simmer for 25 minutes, or until the liquid has evaporated and the rice is just tender.

3 While the rice is cooking, make a marinade by combining the olive oil, herbs, garlic, and Bragg in a blender.

So you can see the challenge that lies ahead in recreating this traditional Spanish treasure. The ingredients are extensive for this recipe, but for anyone who loves paella, you know it is worth the effort. The resulting recipe is a mouthwatering delight to our guests. The only thing missing is a nice sangria!

4 Lightly oil 2 cookie sheets with canola oil, and place the squash and peppers on one sheet. On the other sheet, place the eggplant and mushrooms, cap side up. Using a pastry brush, brush the marinade on all the vegetables except the red peppers.

5 Place the tray of eggplant and mushrooms on the top oven rack. Broil for 12 minutes or until the eggplant is lightly browned. Remove and allow to cool. Repeat with the tray of peppers and squash, broiling for 15 minutes or until the peppers are charred and the squash is lightly browned. Set aside to cool.

6 Brown the vegetarian sausage according to package directions, being sure to brown the sausage on all sides. Allow to cool slightly.

7 Remove the skins from the peppers, and cut all the vegetables into 1-inch chunks.

8 Slice the sausage diagonally. Toss the cubed vegetables, sausage, and vegetarian pepperoni together. Place on a cookie sheet, and heat in a 450°F oven for about 3 to 5 minutes until hot.

9 In a large bowl, fold the rice, baby peas, and vegetables together. Place in a large 10 x 13-inch casserole dish, and heat in the oven for a few minutes to insure everything is hot.

Per serving: Calories 305, Protein 10 g, Fat 10 g, Carbohydrate 42 g, Fiber 5 g, Calcium 31 mg, Sodium 479 mg

Kale and Mushroom Casserole

Yield: 6 to 8 servings

This dish was a big hit the very first time we tried it. Try replacing the kale with any of your favorite greens.

1 bunch kale, stems removed and cut

1 bunch turnip greens, chopped
(Frozen greens are fine.)

1 teaspoon olive oil

1 large yellow or Vidalia onion,
chopped

1 tablespoon minced garlic

8 ounces button mushrooms, cut in
half

4 portobello mushrooms, stems and
gills removed, sliced

One 12.3-ounce box firm silken tofu

1 tablespoon Bragg Liquid Aminos

6 ounces soy mozzarella, shredded

1 cup whole wheat bread crumbs

2 teaspoons olive oil

2 teaspoons dried oregano

Per serving: Calories 196, Protein 13 g,
Fat 8 g, Carbohydrate 18 g, Fiber 4 g,
Calcium 245 mg, Sodium 360 mg

1 Preheat the oven to 400°F.

2 Steam the greens until tender.
Squeeze the greens to remove
the liquid.

3 In a large sauté pan, heat the oil
and sauté the onion and garlic
until golden. Add the mushrooms,
cover, and simmer until tender.

4 Drain some of the juice from the
mushrooms, and place in a blender
with the tofu and Bragg, and purée.

5 Combine the mushrooms, greens,
and tofu mixture together in a large
bowl with half of the soy cheese.

6 Place the vegetable mix in an
appropriate size casserole dish.

7 In a small bowl, combine the
bread crumbs, oil, remaining
cheese, and oregano. Sprinkle the
mixture over the greens, mix,
and bake on the top rack for 20
to 25 minutes, or until the top is
a golden brown.

MEATLESS CHILI

Yield: 6 to 8 servings

The day we prepared this chili for the first time, the entire kitchen staff and our resident taste–tester Julio DiIorio looked at each other in amazement; like we had discovered the Vegetarian Holy Grail! Chili was once again back in our lives. This chili can be served as an entree, as part of a taco salad bar with tortilla chips, as a topping for pizzas, or as a filling for burritos, tacos, enchiladas, or wherever your creativity will take you.

1 yellow onion, chopped

1 tablespoon minced garlic

1 red bell pepper, chopped

1 yellow bell pepper, chopped

1 tablespoon extra-virgin olive oil, or
   2 tablespoons vegetable broth

Two 12-ounce packages Boca Ground
   Burger or other vegetarian crumbles

One 16-ounce can diced tomatoes, or
   2 cups fresh diced tomatoes

1 cup tomato purée

One 16-ounce can cooked pinto or
   kidney beans, drained

Dash of cayenne pepper

3 tablespoons chili powder

1 to 2 teaspoons ground cumin

1 teaspoon ground oregano

1 bay leaf

1 Sauté the onions, garlic, and peppers in the olive oil or broth until lightly browned, then add the crumbled vegetarian burger and stir until heated through.

2 Add the remaining ingredients, cover, and simmer for about 1 hour. Adjust the seasonings to taste.

Per serving: Calories 248, Protein 29 g, Fat 3 g, Carbohydrate 36 g, Fiber 13 g, Calcium 96 mg, Sodium 477 mg

Pastelon

Yield: 6 to 8 servings

I first had this delicious casserole while vacationing in Puerto Rico. It is made with ripe plantains (Caribbean bananas) and an unusual chili called picadillo, which is made with olives and raisins.

4 very ripe plantains (almost black in color)

1 tablespoon canola oil

1 quart Picadillo, page 168

Per serving: Calories 256, Protein 9 g, Fat 3 g, Carbohydrate 46 g, Fiber 5 g, Calcium 53 mg, Sodium 193 mg

1 Preheat the oven to 375°F.

2 Peel the plantains and slice lengthwise ½ inch thick.

3 Heat the canola oil in a large sauté pan or electric griddle. Lay the plantain pieces flat in the pan, and brown on both sides. Lay the browned plantains on a paper towel to absorb some of the oil.

4 Place an even layer of plantains in the bottom of an 8 x 8-inch casserole dish.

5 Spoon an even layer of picadillo over the plantains.

6 Cover the top of the picadillo with another even layer of the plantains. Bake on the bottom rack of the oven for 35 to 40 minutes, or until hot and bubbly.

7 Remove the casserole and allow to cool for about 5 minutes before cutting into squares. Use two spatulas to remove from the dish, one to lift from the casserole and one to push onto the plates.

RATATOUILLE

This French vegetable stew is great with a whole wheat baguette or served over brown rice. Don't be put off by the long list of ingredients. Once you prepare all of your vegetables, the rest of the recipe is easy to complete.

2 red bell peppers

2 yellow bell peppers

1 small eggplant

2 zucchini

2 yellow squash

2 yellow or Vidalia onions

4 large vine-ripe tomatoes

8 ounces button or shiitake mushrooms

1 tablespoon extra-virgin olive oil

2 tablespoons minced garlic

One 16-ounce can tomato purée

2 tablespoons chopped fresh oregano, or 2 teaspoons dried

2 tablespoons chopped fresh basil

1 tablespoon chopped fresh thyme

2 bay leaves

½ teaspoon sea salt (optional)

Dash of cayenne pepper

Per serving: Calories 177, Protein 5 g, Fat 3 g, Carbohydrate 32 g, Fiber 9 g, Calcium 66 mg, Sodium 61 mg

1 If time allows, roast the bell peppers and peel the skins.

2 Seed the bell peppers and peel the eggplant. Cut the ends off the zucchini and squash, and cut in half lengthwise. Peel the onion and core the tomatoes. Cut all into 1-inch cubes. Discard the stems of any shiitake mushrooms, and cut the mushrooms in half.

3 In a large pot, heat the olive oil and sauté the onions and garlic until golden brown.

4 Add the peppers, eggplant, zucchini, and squash, and continue cooking for about 5 minutes, stirring occasionally.

5 Add the chopped tomatoes, tomato purée, mushrooms, herbs, and spices, and simmer for about 45 minutes.

6 Adjust the seasonings to taste, and stir occasionally.

Refried Beans

Yield: approximately 1½ quarts

This versatile dish can be used as hummus, for filling in enchiladas and burritos, in a 5–layer dip, and many more creative ways. To save time, you may use canned kidney beans and season and prepare as below. You can also substitute other bean varieties such as pinto or black beans.

1 pound kidney beans

2½ quarts distilled or pure water

2 bay leaves

2 tablespoons minced garlic

1 Vidalia or yellow onion, chopped

1 red bell pepper, chopped

1 yellow or orange bell pepper, chopped

2 tablespoons ground cumin

Dash of cayenne pepper

2 tablespoons Bragg Liquid Aminos

Per ½ cup: Calories 58, Protein 3 g, Fat 0 g, Carbohydrate 11 g, Fiber 2 g, Calcium 15 mg, Sodium 112 mg

1 Soak the kidney beans in enough scalding water to cover for 1 to 2 hours, then drain.

2 In a large pot, bring the distilled water to a boil. Add the beans, bay leaves, and garlic, and simmer for 1 hour.

3 Add all the remaining ingredients, and simmer for 1 hour or until the beans are tender. Adjust the seasonings to taste.

4 While the beans are still hot, remove the bay leaves and purée the beans in a food processor or in batches in a blender with a little bit of the cooking liquid until creamy.

Risotto with Wild Mushrooms

Yield: 4 servings

This creamy rice dish goes well with grilled or steamed vegetables. Cooking risotto is different than for traditional rice, because you can stir it while the liquid is reducing and can watch the beauty of the dish unfold. Feel free to experiment with other mushroom varieties that you enjoy.

8 ounces shiitake mushrooms, stems removed and set aside

1½ quarts vegetable broth

2 teaspoons olive oil

4 scallions, sliced ¼ inch thick

1 tablespoon minced garlic

⅓ cup white wine or vegetable broth

2 teaspoons minced fresh thyme, or 1 tablespoon other chopped fresh herbs

1 tablespoon Bragg Liquid Aminos

Dash of cayenne pepper, or ⅛ teaspoon ground black pepper

2 cups short grain brown rice or arborio rice

2 cups fresh or frozen baby peas or sugar snap peas

Per serving: Calories 326, Protein 8 g, Fat 4 g, Carbohydrate 62 g, Fiber 6 g, Calcium 64 mg, Sodium 175 mg

1 Simmer the reserved mushroom stems in the 1½ quarts vegetable broth for 15 to 20 minutes.

2 Heat the oil in a large, heavy-bottomed saucepan. Add the scallions and garlic, and sauté for 3 to 5 minutes until lightly golden.

3 Add the mushrooms, wine or ⅓ cup broth, herbs, Bragg, and cayenne, and simmer 1 minute.

4 Stir in the rice and add 2 cups of the hot vegetable broth. Discard mushroom stems before adding the broth. Continue stirring the rice until the broth is absorbed.

5 Add 2 more cups of hot broth, and continue stirring until it is absorbed.

6 Fold in the peas and add the remaining hot broth. Continue stirring slowly until the broth has been absorbed, and serve.

Savory Lentil Loaf

Yield: 6 to 8 servings

This nutritious version of meat loaf is low-fat, high-protein, and full of flavor. Serve with a marinara or wild mushroom sauce and mashed potatoes.

3 cups pure or distilled water

1½ cup green or pink lentils, rinsed

2 tablespoons Bragg Liquid Aminos

2 teaspoons ground cumin

Dash of cayenne pepper

1 Vidalia or yellow onion, chopped

1 teaspoon canola oil

1 tablespoon minced garlic

1 red bell pepper, chopped

¾ cup cooked brown rice

¾ cup rolled oats

1 cup drained cooked corn

Per serving: Calories 294, Protein 14 g
Fat 2 g, Carbohydrate 53 g, Fiber 8 g,
Calcium 47 mg, Sodium 6 mg

1 Place the water, lentils, Bragg, cumin, and pepper in a pot, and bring to a medium boil.

2 Cook until the lentils are tender and the liquid has evaporated.

3 Sauté the onions in the canola oil until brown. Add the garlic and peppers, and cook until tender.

4 Place the lentils, vegetables, and remaining ingredients in a large bowl, and mix together thoroughly.

5 Preheat the oven to 375°F. Oil a loaf pan completely with canola oil.

6 Pack the lentil mixture evenly into the loaf pan, and bake for 35 to 40 minutes.

7 Remove the loaf from the oven. Insert a knife around the edge of the loaf, and trim around the pan for easy removal. Cut into ¾-inch-thick slices, and serve.

Soy "Picadillo"

Yield: 3 to 4 servings

This Latin chili recipe tastes as good as the original version, without the ground beef of course. You can serve this dish alone, over rice, with pasta, or as a topping for a baked potato. Another way to use picadillo is as a filling for a Puerto Rican specialty called pastelon, a casserole made with ripened plantains. See the recipe for it on page 168.

1 teaspoon canola oil

1 large Vidalia or yellow onion, chopped

1 large red or yellow bell pepper, chopped

1 tablespoon minced garlic

2 tablespoons whole wheat pastry flour

3 tablespoons chili powder

1 teaspoon ground cumin

2 cups vegetable broth or water

½ cup tomato purée

1 tablespoon low-sodium tamari

1¼ cups textured soy protein granules

½ cup raisins

½ cup sliced green olives

Per serving: Calories 228, Protein 17 g, Fat 3 g, Carbohydrate 34 g, Fiber 6 g, Calcium 101 mg, Sodium 379 mg

1 Heat the canola oil in a large pot. Add the onions and sauté until golden. Add the peppers and garlic, and continue to cook a few more minutes.

2 Turn the heat to low. Combine the flour, chili powder, and cumin, and sprinkle into the vegetable mixture very slowly and evenly. If you add this too quickly, you may have lumps in your sauce.

3 Whip in the vegetable broth, tomato purée, and tamari. Simmer until thickened.

4 Add the textured soy granules, raisins, and olives, and simmer for 10 to 12 minutes until the granules are as tender as you like them. Adjust the seasonings to taste, and serve.

Stuffed Cabbage Roll (Golomki)

Yield: 4 to 6 servings

Being Polish, I remember dining on my mother's delicious golomki as an experience I will cherish forever. When my mother asked me if I had a meatless version of her classic specialty, I felt it an honor to recreate it "vegan–style."

1 large green cabbage, cored and rinsed (1½ to 2 pounds)

1 teaspoon canola oil

1 pound crumbled vegetarian burger

Tomato Sauce

2 teaspoons vegetable broth or extra-virgin olive oil

1 large Vidalia or yellow onion, chopped

1 red bell pepper, chopped

1 tablespoon minced garlic

One 12-ounce can diced tomatoes, or 1½ cups fresh diced tomatoes

One 12-ounce can tomato purée

1 tablespoon coarsely chopped fresh basil

2 bay leaves

½ cup brown rice syrup (optional)

Dash of cayenne pepper

½ teaspoon sea salt (optional)

2 cups cooked brown rice

1 Place the cabbage in about 1 quart of hot water in a large, deep pot. Cover and steam on medium-high heat for about 30 minutes until the cabbage is tender. Place the cabbage carefully in a strainer, and allow to cool while preparing the other ingredients.

2 Oil a sauté pan with the canola oil, and cook the vegetarian burger until browned; set aside.

3 To prepare the tomato sauce, heat the broth or olive oil and lightly brown the onion, pepper, and garlic in a large pot.

4 Add the diced tomato, tomato purée, basil, bay leaves, brown rice syrup, and cayenne, and cook for 20 to 30 minutes until the flavors have blended. Adjust the seasonings to tastes.

5 Transfer the vegetarian burger mix to a large bowl, and fold in 1 cup of the tomato sauce and the cooked rice. Allow to cool slightly.

6 Preheat the oven to 400°F. Place about 1½ cups of tomato sauce in the bottom of a 9 x 13-inch, or 3-quart, casserole dish.

7 Gently remove the cabbage leaves one at a time until the leaves are too small to use for stuffing. You may julienne the remaining cabbage and add to the side of the casserole.

8 Place one cabbage leaf on a plate, and spoon about ⅓ cup of the burger and rice mixture in the center of the leaf. Starting nearest you, begin to roll the cabbage over the filling while also tucking the sides of the leaves to close. When fully rolled, place in the casserole dish seam side down to ensure it doesn't open.

9 Complete the remaining cabbage rolls, and place side by side in the casserole. Cover with some of the tomato sauce.

10 Cover the casserole dish with plastic wrap, then with foil, and bake 45 minutes until well steamed.

11 Serve with the remaining sauce. Leftovers may be frozen for serving later and reheated with no loss of quality.

Per serving: Calories 226, Protein 14 g, Fat 2 g, Carbohydrate 39 g, Fiber 7 g, Calcium 122 mg, Sodium 55 mg

BOCA BURGER STUFFED PEPPERS WITH BROWN RICE

Yield: 6 to 8 servings

I developed this recipe for the Boca Burger company to be used with their vegetarian ground burger product. Outstanding!

1 teaspoon canola oil

12 ounces Boca Ground Burger

2 yellow or orange bell peppers

2 red bell peppers

1 Heat the canola oil in a sauté pan, add the ground burger, and cook until browned. Set aside

2 Rinse the bell peppers. Cut in half lengthwise, seed, and set aside.

3 Prepare the tomato sauce by heating the broth or olive oil in a 3-quart pot, adding the onion, pepper, and garlic, and lightly browning.

4 Add the diced tomato, tomato puree, basil, bay leaves, brown rice syrup, if using, and cayenne, and cook for 20 to 30 minutes until the flavors have blended. Adjust the seasonings to taste.

5 Transfer the ground burger to a large bowl, and fold in 1 cup of the tomato sauce and the cooked riced. Allow to cool slightly.

Tomato Sauce

2 tablespoons vegetable broth or
extra-virgin olive oil

2 large Vidalia or yellow onions,
chopped

1 red bell pepper, chopped

2 tablespoons minced garlic

One 12-ounce can diced tomatoes

One 12-ounce can tomato puree

1 tablespoon coarsely chopped basil

2 bay leaves

½ cup brown rice syrup (optional)

Dash of cayenne pepper

½ teaspoon sea salt (optional)

2 cups cooked brown rice

8 ounces soy cheddar or mozzarella,
shredded

Per serving: Calories 282, Protein 19 g,
Fat 9 g, Carbohydrate 34 g, Fiber 7 g,
Calcium 80 mg, Sodium 527 mg

6 Preheat the oven to 400°F. Place
about 1½ cups of the tomato
sauce in the bottom of a 9 X 13-
inch (or 3-quart) casserole dish.

7 Fill the peppers with the rice
and ground burger mixture.

8 Cover the casserole dish with
plastic wrap, then with foil, and
bake for 45 minutes until the
peppers are well steamed.

9 Remove the casserole dish from
the oven, and sprinkle the peppers with the cheese. Bake uncovered for about 10 minutes more,
until the cheese has melted.

10 Remove the peppers from the
oven, and serve with the remaining sauce.

VEGETABLE CHILI

Yield: 6 to 8 servings

This is one of my favorite chilis to prepare. It tastes even better the next day. We always use organic beans and cook and season them from scratch. However, the canned beans used here will save you a great deal of time and effort. If time allows, try roasting the peppers first for better flavor.

This chili is wonderful with corn bread and brown rice or quinoa pilaf, or garnish with shredded soy cheese. It will keep for 5 to 7 days in the refrigerator.

2 yellow or Vidalia onions

2 red bell peppers

2 yellow or orange bell peppers

1 small eggplant, unpeeled

2 zucchini

2 yellow squash

3 large vine-ripe tomatoes, cored, or one 16-ounce can diced tomatoes

1 tablespoon olive oil

2 tablespoons minced garlic

One 12-ounce can tomato purée

3 tablespoons chili powder

1 Cut all the vegetables into 1-inch cubes.

2 In a large pot, heat the olive oil and sauté the onions and garlic until golden brown.

3 Add the peppers, eggplant, zucchini, and squash, and continue cooking until slightly tender.

2 tablespoons ground cumin

2 tablespoons chopped fresh cilantro

2 bay leaves

½ teaspoon sea salt (optional)

1 jalapeño pepper, with seeds removed, very finely chopped (for note on handling hot peppers, see page 12)

One 15-ounce can kidney or pinto beans

One 15-ounce can black beans

Per serving: Calories 253, Protein 11 g, Fat 2 g, Carbohydrate 46 g, Fiber 10 g, Calcium 84 mg, Sodium 32 mg

4 Add the diced tomato and purée, chili powder, cumin, cilantro, bay leaves, and salt, and continue cooking until well blended.

5 Drain the liquid from the canned beans, and fold into the vegetable mixture. Cover and simmer for 30 to 45 minutes, stirring occasionally.

6 Adjust the seasonings to taste.

Vegetable Pita Pizza

Yield: 4 to 6 servings

This low-fat recipe will appeal to kids as well as adults. Other suggestions to create your own personalized gourmet pizza: sun-dried tomatoes, imported sliced olives, roasted red peppers, sautéed onions, sautéed wild mushrooms, grilled eggplant, or vegetarian chili.

Three 8-inch whole wheat pitas (Smaller pitas will also work), or Focaccia, page 94-95

2 tablespoons extra-virgin olive oil

2 teaspoons minced garlic

2 teaspoons minced fresh oregano

2 large vine-ripe tomatoes, chopped

Dash of cayenne pepper

1 pound fresh spinach or 1 head romaine or escarole, rinsed, stems removed, and drained

8 ounces mushrooms, washed and sliced ¼ inch thick

One 16-ounce can artichoke hearts, drained and sliced (optional)

12 ounces soy mozzarella, shredded (fat-free if available)

Per serving: Calories 202, Protein 11 g, Fat 6 g, Carbohydrate 21 g, Fiber 6 g, Calcium 445 mg, Sodium 405 mg

1 Preheat the oven to 400°F.

2 Split the pitas in half with a serrated knife to resemble pizza shells.

3 Purée the olive oil and half of the garlic and oregano in a blender.

4 With a pastry brush, brush the inside of the pita halves lightly with the olive oil mix.

5 Bake the pitas on a baking sheet for 6 to 8 minutes until golden brown and crispy. Set aside to cool.

6 Combine the tomatoes with the remaining garlic, oregano, and cayenne.

7 Lay the pitas on a clean surface with the inside half facing upward. Cover completely with the spinach leaves, then a layer of mushrooms, tomatoes, and artichokes.

8 Cover with the soy mozzarella, and bake on the top oven rack for 6 to 8 minutes, or until the cheese is melted completely.

POTATO
Dishes

Baked Potatoes

Whether it is an Idaho potato, sweet potato, or yam, our guests always tell us that our potatoes taste so much better than theirs do back home. I humbly comment, "Things tend to taste better when someone else is cooking for you." But some still think that there is a secret to potato baking. Well, here is our not–so–secret recipe for baked potatoes. If none of these ideas make your potatoes as good as those served at the Regency House Spa, I guess the real secret must be the salty ocean air and peaceful ambiance of our little gem of a spa.

1 Preheat the oven to 400°F.

2 Scrub the potatoes under cool running water with a brush or nylon pot scrubber. You may also want to add a drop of non-toxic soap to some water, scrub the potatoes with that, and rinse again.

3 Place the potatoes directly on the bottom oven rack, and bake for 1 hour. That's it!

Tips

✳ Resist the urge to wrap the potatoes in foil. This will make the skin limp and chewy and the flesh will be dense and moist. Rubbing potatoes with oil will produce a similar steamed effect, but is not necessary at all. You may choose to prick your potatoes beforehand with a fork, which will allow the steam to escape with excellent results.

✳ If you are not serving your potatoes immediately, reduce the oven to 225°F to keep the potatoes warm until needed. I do not recommend doing this longer than 20 to 30 minutes or the potatoes will turn mushy. Idaho potatoes will become starchy, yellow, and lose their flavor.

✳ When baking sweet potatoes, line the base of your oven with foil or place a disposable foil baking sheet on the oven rack below them to catch the drippings.

✳ If you are in a hurry and must use the microwave, here is an alternative "quickie" recipe. Microwave the potatoes for 5 minutes, and preheat the oven to 400°F. Remove the potatoes and place directly on the bottom oven rack for 8 to 10 minutes until the skin is crispy the way you like it. Serve immediately.

Per potato: **Calories 220, Protein 3 g, Fat 0 g, Carbohydrate 51 g, Fiber 5 g, Calcium 20 mg, Sodium 16 mg**

Low-fat Baked Potato Skins

Yield: 3 to 4 servings

This is a much more nutritious, lower-fat version of popular fried potato skins.

4 Idaho baking potatoes

4 ounces soy cheddar or mozzarella

3 scallions or chives, thinly sliced

¾ cup crumbled cooked vegetarian bacon (optional)

1 cup soy sour cream or rice sour cream (optional)

Per serving: Calories 290, Protein 11 g, Fat 4 g, Carbohydrate 52 g, Fiber 5 g, Calcium 150 mg, Sodium 196 mg

1 Preheat the oven to 400°F.

2 Scrub the potatoes, place them directly on an oven rack, and bake for 1 hour.

3 Remove the potatoes to cool. Shred the cheese and mince the scallions.

4 Cut the potatoes in half lengthwise, and scoop out ⅔ of the pulp.

5 Lay the potatoes skin side down in a baking pan. Sprinkle with the crumbled vegetarian bacon, if using, and cover generously with the shredded cheese.

6 Return to the oven and bake on the top oven rack for 8 to 10 minutes, or until the cheese melts.

7 Garnish with the scallions, and serve with soy sour cream, if desired.

Champs Elysées Potatoes

Yield: 6 to 8 servings

This casserole was created by Escoffier, the father of French cooking, for the dedication of the world-famous Paris boulevard of the same name. Quite a tasty combination of potatoes, cheese, and mushrooms.

4 large Idaho potatoes

1 teaspoon olive oil

1 tablespoon soy margarine

1 onion, chopped

1 tablespoon minced garlic

1 pound button mushrooms, sliced

½ teaspoon sea salt (optional)

¼ teaspoon ground black pepper

12 ounces soy cheddar, shredded

1 Peel the potatoes and shred on the large side of a grater. Place in cool water to prevent discoloration.

2 Preheat the oven to 400°F.

Per serving: Calories 249, Protein 8 g, Fat 2 g, Carbohydrate 46 g, Fiber 5 g, Calcium 259 mg, Sodium 359 mg

3 Heat the oil and margarine in a sauté pan, add the onions, and cook about 3 minutes. Add the garlic and continue to sauté until lightly brown.

4 Add the mushrooms, salt, and pepper, and cook about 5 minutes. Drain off the liquid.

5 Pour the shredded potatoes into a colander, and squeeze out as much liquid as possible.

6 Lightly oil or rub some soy margarine on the inside of an 8 x 8-inch casserole dish.

7 Place a ½-inch layer of the potatoes in the bottom of the casserole.

8 Sprinkle a layer of mushrooms over the potatoes followed by a layer of cheese. Finish with a layer of potatoes, a layer of mushrooms, and a generous layer of cheese.

9 Place the casserole on the bottom oven rack, and bake for 25 to 30 minutes, or until the cheese is bubbling and lightly golden. Cut into squares. To make serving easier, use two spatulas, one to scoop out the potatoes and one to slide them onto the plate.

Duchess Potatoes

Yield: 8 to 10 servings

Here is an opportunity to work on your pastry bag skills. Basically, this French potato classic is mashed potatoes with eggs and cream added. Of course, we have found a way to make it cholesterol-free.

You can pipe the potatoes as a plate garnish or a casserole border for au gratin vegetables or Coquille St. Jacques. You may also try making "baby duchess potatoes" by making smaller circles and not mounding them quite as high.

4 Idaho potatoes

⅔ cup rice milk, soymilk, or oat milk

½ teaspoon sea salt (optional)

2 tablespoons chopped chives (optional)

⅛ teaspoon nutmeg

Dash of cayenne pepper or other ground pepper

3 ounces soy cheddar or other nondairy cheese, shredded

Per serving: Calories 110, Protein 4 g, Fat 2 g, Carbohydrate 20 g, Fiber 2 g, Calcium 51 mg, Sodium 64 mg

1 Peel the potatoes, cut into 1-inch cubes, and set in a bowl of in cool water to keep from discoloring. Try to time the cooking of the potatoes with the heating of the rice milk or soymilk in Step 4. Do not allow the potatoes to cool down. This will cause more lumps when you mash them and make it difficult to pipe through the pastry bag.

2 Bring a large pot of water to a boil, and cook the potatoes about 15 to 18 minutes, or until tender. Drain the potatoes in a colander, and either return them to the pot or put them in a large bowl. Preheat the oven to 425°F.

3 While the potatoes are cooking, heat the rice milk or other alternative, salt, chives, nutmeg, and pepper in a saucepan until just scalding; do not boil.

4 Mash the potatoes and drizzle in the rice milk mixture until the potatoes have become somewhat creamy, but not runny.

5 Fold the shredded cheese into the potato mixture. Lightly oil a baking sheet with canola oil.

6 Place a large, widely opened rosette tip into the end of a large pastry bag, and place a few large spoonfuls of potato mix in the bag. Do not over-fill the bag.

7 Twist the top end of the pastry bag to close it, and slowly pipe the potatoes into a 3-inch circle. As you complete the circle base, slowly continue piping in a circular motion a few more times around until you reach the top. Be careful not to make it too high or it may topple over. Sprinkle a little paprika or Parmesan cheese over to garnish. Continue piping the potatoes and refilling the bag until finished. Leave a little space between each potato.

8 Bake on the bottom rack of the oven for 15 to 18 minutes until lightly browned. Serve with a metal spatula for best results.

Lyonnaise Potatoes

Yield: 3 to 4 servings

Lyonnaise is a French term for food that is accompanied by onions. It is derived from the city of Lyons, which has a renowned gastronomic tradition. I prefer Red Bliss potatoes in this recipe for their quality, color, and the fact that you do not have to peel them—which means less work for the chef of the house. These potatoes are great for breakfast, lunch, or dinner. We serve it with our tofu quiche, scrambled tofu, or with a variety of steamed vegetables.

1 pound Red Bliss potatoes or other new red potatoes

1 teaspoon canola oil

1 tablespoon soy margarine

1 large yellow or white onion, thinly sliced

1 tablespoon minced garlic (optional)

½ teaspoon sea salt (optional)

¼ teaspoon freshly ground black pepper (optional)

½ teaspoon paprika (optional)

Per serving: Calories 169, Protein 2 g, Fat 5 g, Carbohydrate 30 g, Fiber 3 g, Calcium 19 mg, Sodium 45 mg

1 Scrub the potatoes and slice ½ inch thick. Place the sliced potatoes in a bowl of cool water to prevent discoloration.

2 Bring a pot of water to a boil, drain the potatoes, and cook for about 5 minutes. Pour the blanched potatoes into a colander to drain again.

3 Heat the oil and margarine in a large sauté pan. Add the onions and sauté on medium-high heat for about 5 minutes, stirring occasionally, until lightly browned.

4 Add the garlic and continue to cook for a minute or two.

5 Add the cooked potatoes and optional seasonings, and toss well with the onions.

6 Continue to cook over medium heat until the potatoes are tender.

Oven-Browned Herbed New Potatoes

Yield: 6 to 8 servings

These potatoes are great for breakfast, lunch, or dinner.

8 new potatoes

2 tablespoons extra-virgin olive oil

2 teaspoons minced garlic

2 tablespoons chopped fresh parsley

1 tablespoon chopped fresh thyme or rosemary

½ teaspoon sea salt (optional)

⅔ cup grated soy Parmesan

Per serving: Calories 203, Protein 7 g, Fat 5 g, Carbohydrate 32 g, Fiber 3 g, Calcium 8 mg, Sodium 214 mg

1 Preheat the oven to 425°F.

2 Scrub the potatoes under cold running water. Cut in quarters and cover with cool water.

3 Whip together in a blender the olive oil with the garlic, parsley, thyme or rosemary, and salt. Drain the potatoes thoroughly in a colander.

4 Toss the oil mixture with the potatoes, and spread out on a baking sheet.

5 Bake for about 45 minutes to 1 hour. Remove from the oven and sprinkle with the soy Parmesan. Return to the top rack of the oven for about 10 minutes, or until the Parmesan is slightly browned and crispy.

Oven-fried Sweet Potato Spears

Yield: 4 servings

Caution: It is a good idea to prepare extra of these, or you may run out quickly! For a more caramelized flavor bake longer, being careful not to burn.

4 unpeeled sweet potatoes

¼ cup extra-virgin olive oil

1 teaspoon minced garlic

2 teaspoons chopped fresh thyme or rosemary

2 teaspoons chopped fresh basil or oregano

Per serving: Calories 277, Protein 2 g, Fat 13 g, Carbohydrate 38 g, Fiber 3 g, Calcium 18 mg, Sodium 12 mg

1 Preheat the oven to 425°F.

2 Scrub the sweet potatoes under cold running water. Cut in half lengthwise, then cut into wedges ¾ inch thick.

3 Whip together the olive oil, garlic, and herbs in a blender or in a bowl.

4 Toss the oil mixture with the sweet potatoes, and place the potatoes on a baking sheet.

5 Bake for 45 minutes to 1 hour on the top rack of the oven, or until tender and a little charred.

Twice-stuffed Baked Potatoes

Yield: 6 servings

At the tender age of 16, I was the chef of Smitty's Steak and Lobster in my hometown of Baltimore, Maryland. I made hundreds of "Jack Tar" stuffed potatoes with bacon pieces, sour cream, and cheddar cheese. This vegetarian recipe tastes exactly like the ones I made years ago . . . except healthier, of course!

3 large Idaho baking potatoes, scrubbed

6 new red potatoes, scrubbed and quartered

2 quarts pure or distilled water

1 cup rice milk or soymilk, scalded

4 slices vegetarian bacon, baked and crumbled

3 scallions, minced

3 tablespoons rice or soy sour cream (optional)

1 tablespoon minced garlic

½ teaspoon sea salt (optional)

Dash of cayenne pepper

2 ounces soy cheddar, shredded

2 tablespoons grated soy Parmesan (optional)

Per serving: Calories 296, Protein 8 g, Fat 2 g, Carbohydrate 60 g, Fiber 7 g, Calcium 96 mg, Sodium 181 mg

1 Preheat the oven to 400°F. Bake the Idaho potatoes for 1 hour. Set the baked potatoes aside to cool.

2 Bring the water to a boil. Boil the new potatoes until very tender. Drain and either return the potatoes to the pot or a mixing bowl.

3 Preheat the oven to 400°F again. Cut the baked potatoes lengthwise, and scoop out the pulp.

4 Add the potato pulp, rice milk, scallions, sour cream, garlic, salt, and cayenne to the red potato mix, and mash with a potato masher or mixer.

5 Fill the baked potato shells with the potato mix, and top with the cheeses.

6 Bake for 18 to 20 minutes, or until the cheese is melted, and serve hot.

Scalloped Potatoes

Yield: 4 servings

When the owner of the Regency Spa, Mr. Nick Dejnega, had a craving for scalloped potatoes, that was all the challenge I needed to create a nutritious vegetarian version of the original dish.

3 Idaho potatoes

One 12.3-ounce box extra-firm silken tofu or soft regular tofu

1 teaspoon minced garlic

2 teaspoons yellow miso, or ¼ teaspoon sea salt (optional)

Dash of ground nutmeg

Dash of cayenne pepper or freshly ground black pepper

½ cup soy or rice Parmesan

Per serving: Calories 262, Protein 15 g, Fat 4 g, Carbohydrate 42 g, Fiber 5 g, Calcium 39 mg, Sodium 317 mg

1 Peel the potatoes and slice slowly and carefully ¼ inch thick with a sharp knife. That will insure uniform slices and (more importantly) prevent you from slicing your finger. Place the potatoes in cool water to prevent discoloration.

2 Preheat the oven to 425°F. Bring a pot of water to a boil to cook the potatoes.

3 Drain the water from the potatoes, and partially cook them for about 6 to 8 minutes.

4 Pour the potatoes carefully into a colander to avoid breaking them up.

5 Make a cream sauce by processing the tofu, garlic, miso or salt, nutmeg, and pepper in a blender until smooth.

6 Lightly oil the bottom of an 8 x 8-inch casserole dish. Layer the potatoes overlapping in straight lines across the bottom of the casserole.

7 Pour the cream sauce evenly over the potatoes until they are reasonably well covered.

8 Sprinkle the soy Parmesan generously over the potatoes along the same lines that you have laid out the potatoes.

9 Place the casserole on the top rack of the oven, and bake for 30 to 35 minutes, or until the cheese is golden and the potatoes are tender. You can use a fork or knife to test.

Shepherd's Pie

Yield: 8 servings

You will love this vegan twist to an old favorite, cholesterol–free and much lower in fat. Substitute parboiled broccoli and carrot pieces for the vegetarian burger, if you want a less hearty dish.

For a decorative touch, you can also garnish the pie with extra mashed potatoes around the perimeter of the pan if you have a pastry bag and a large rosette tip. The Wild Mushroom Sauce on page 70 is a wonderful accompaniment to this dish.

1 teaspoon canola oil, or ¼ cup vegetable broth

1 large yellow onion, chopped

2 teaspoons minced garlic

8 ounces sliced mushrooms (optional)

12 ounces Boca Ground Burger

1 red bell pepper, chopped

2 tablespoons Bragg Liquid Aminos

Dash of cayenne pepper

2 cups cooked corn

1 Heat the oil or ¼ cup broth in a large sauté pan. Add the onions and 2 teaspoons garlic, and either brown slightly or steam until tender. Add the mushrooms and cook for 3 minutes.

2 Add the ground burger, red pepper and dash of cayenne. Simmer for 10 minutes, then add the corn and cover. Lower the heat to warm, and let sit.

3 Bring a pot of water to a boil, and cook the potatoes until tender.

4 Drain the potatoes, add the rice milk or soymilk, miso, 1 tablespoon garlic, and the remaining dash of cayenne, and mash thoroughly.

4 large, unpeeled red potatoes, quartered

1 cup rice milk, soymilk, or oat milk, scalded

1 tablespoon yellow miso

1 tablespoon minced garlic

Dash of cayenne pepper

Paprika, for garnish

Per serving: Calories 196, Protein 11 g, Fat 3 g, Carbohydrate 34 g, Fiber 5 g, Calcium 44 mg, Sodium 421 mg

5 Preheat the oven to 400°F.

6 Spread the burger mix evenly in a 10 x 13-inch casserole, and cover with the mashed potatoes.

7 Dust the top with paprika, and bake on the top rack of the oven for about 35 to 40 minutes, or until slightly browned.

8 Remove from the oven and serve hot, cutting with a metal spatula to get uniform pieces.

Sweet Potato Soufflé

Yield: 6 to 8 servings

This egg–free soufflé can be enjoyed year round. You may not be able to wait for a holiday to come once you have tried this recipe.

4 large sweet potatoes, peeled and cut into quarters

⅔ cup rice milk, soymilk, or almond milk, scalded

2 teaspoons ground cinnamon

1 teaspoon ground nutmeg

½ cup brown rice syrup or maple syrup

⅔ cup chopped pecans

1 cup rolled oats

Per serving: Calories 313, Protein 5 g, Fat 7 g, Carbohydrate 57 g, Fiber 5 g, Calcium 25 mg, Sodium 13 mg

1 Bring a pot of water to a boil, and cook the potatoes until they are very tender.

2 Preheat the oven to 400°F.

3 Drain the potatoes and transfer to a large mixing bowl.

4 Mash the potatoes with the rice milk and half of the cinnamon and nutmeg.

5 Place the potato mixture in a 10 x 13-inch casserole dish, and smooth over with a spatula.

6 In a small bowl, toss the remaining cinnamon and nutmeg with the pecans and oatmeal.

7 Add the brown rice syrup to the nut mix, and spread evenly over the potatoes. If you desire a sweeter topping, add more syrup.

8 Bake for about 35 to 40 minutes on the top rack of the oven, or until the topping is a little brown and crispy.

Vegetables

Asparagus and Bok Choy Stir-fry

Yield: 4 servings

This is one of my favorite side dishes to prepare. I hope it becomes one of yours as well. Although this recipe is called "stir–fry," we do not heat the oil to sauté. We add toasted sesame oil after the vegetables are cooked for its flavor. Feel free to add any of your other favorite vegetables to this dish, such as carrot or jicama sticks, shiitake mushroom caps, red or yellow bell pepper slices, sliced onions or scallions, water chestnuts, or bamboo shoots.

1 pound fresh asparagus

3 stalks bok choy

2 tablespoons low-sodium tamari or soy sauce

1 teaspoon finely grated ginger

1 teaspoon minced garlic

1 teaspoon toasted sesame oil

1 tablespoon sesame seeds, for garnish

Per serving: Calories 67, Protein 4 g, Fat 2 g, Carbohydrate 7 g, Fiber 3 g, Calcium 125 mg, Sodium 351 mg

1 Trim away the bottoms of the asparagus, and cut the spears into 1-inch pieces. Trim away the greens of the boy choy, and cut the stalks diagonally into ½-inch slices.

Even though the greens are not used in this recipe, you may julienne them and toss them in, or steam or stir-fry them separately with some garlic, sesame oil and a splash of rice vinegar.

2 Toast the sesame seeds in a small sauté pan over medium heat for 3 to 5 minutes until golden brown.

3 Toss the asparagus and bok choy slices together, and steam in enough water to cover them 1 inch for about 3 minutes, or until the asparagus is al dente. Drain away the remaining liquid.

4 While the vegetables are steaming, process the tamari, ginger, garlic, and sesame oil in a blender until smooth.

5 Drizzle a desired amount of the blended mixture over the vegetables. Toss and serve with a toasted sesame seed garnish.

Broccoli Rabe (Rappini)

Yield: 6 to 8 servings

Truly one of the most under–appreciated vegetables, broccoli rabe is dark and leafy with small, soft, broccoli–style florettes attached to thin stems. Without seasoning, it can taste bitter and unpleasant to many. In traditional Italian cuisine, it is served with a squeeze of fresh lemon. I have my own special way of preparing this dish that is so scrumptious I often have it as my main course. Delish! You may also try this recipe with other greens such as Swiss chard, collard greens, kale, or a combination of all of them.

3 bunches broccoli rabe (approximately 1 pound), rinsed in cool water

⅓ cup extra-virgin olive oil

1 tablespoon Bragg Liquid Aminos

2 teaspoons minced garlic

Dash of cayenne pepper

⅓ cup soy or rice Parmesan

Per serving: Calories 120, Protein 4 g, Fat 10 g, Carbohydrate 4 g, Fiber 2 g, Calcium 31 mg, Sodium 210 mg

1 Steam the broccoli rabe in a covered pot in about 1 inch of water for 3 to 5 minutes, or until the thickest stalks are just tender. Turn off the heat and drain the remaining liquid from the pot.

2 While the broccoli rabe is steaming, process the olive oil, Bragg, garlic, and cayenne in the blender until creamy.

3 Drizzle a desired amount of the oil mixture over the broccoli rabe, and toss until well coated. You may need to heat the broccoli rabe a little more.

4 Top the broccoli rabe with a generous amount of soy Parmesan, and serve.

Broccoli with Garlic, Coconut, and Tamari Sauce

Yield: 8 to 10 servings (1 cup sauce)

The tantalizing flavors of the tamari sauce give steamed broccoli a new dimension.

2 heads broccoli

¼ cup low-sodium tamari

¼ cup unsweetened coconut flakes (If using sweetened coconut, taste the sauce before adding the rice syrup.)

¼ cup brown rice syrup

¼ cup pure or distilled water

2 teaspoons minced garlic

Dash of cayenne pepper

2 tablespoons arrowroot

2 tablespoons distilled or pure water

Per serving: Calories 103, Protein 2 g, Fat 4 g, Carbohydrate 14 g, Fiber 3 g, Calcium 40 mg, Sodium 291 mg

1 Remove the outer leaves of the broccoli, and cut into spears. Steam or boil the broccoli 8 to 10 minutes until just tender.

2 Place the remaining ingredients, except the arrowroot and water, in a blender, and process.

3 Combine the arrowroot and water in small bowl, and mix well.

4 Heat the blended mixture in a small pot. When it comes to a boil, whip in the arrowroot mixture, and continue to cook until it makes a thick sauce. If the sauce becomes too thick, add a little more water.

5 Drain the broccoli and spoon on the sauce. Serve hot.

CREAMY CAULIFLOWER AND BABY PEAS

Yield: 4 to 6 servings

The use of rice sour cream in this recipe provides a wonderful nondairy alternative.

1 head cauliflower, cut into florettes

1 cup rice or soy sour cream

½ cup soymilk or rice milk

2 teaspoons minced garlic

2 tablespoons Bragg Liquid Aminos

Dash of cayenne pepper

One 10-ounce package frozen baby peas, lightly steamed

2 tablespoons chopped fresh dill

Per serving: Calories 100, Protein 6 g, Fat 3 g, Carbohydrate 14 g, Fiber 4 g, Calcium 33 mg, Sodium 373 mg

1 Steam or cook the cauliflower for 8 to 10 minutes until just tender.

2 In a large pot, whip together the sour cream, soymilk, garlic, dill, Bragg, and cayenne pepper, and simmer.

3 When the sour cream mix is hot, toss with the cauliflower and peas, and heat for 1 minute.

4 Adjust the spices to taste, and serve hot.

Grilled Eggplant with Roasted Peppers

Yield: 3 to 4 servings

This dish is wonderful as a hot vegetable or chilled as an appetizer salad.

1 eggplant

2 red, orange, or yellow bell peppers

Marinade

⅓ cup pure or distilled water

2 tablespoons extra-virgin olive oil

1 tablespoon chopped fresh basil or oregano

1 teaspoon minced garlic

1 tablespoon Bragg Liquid Aminos

Dash of cayenne pepper

Per serving: Calories 123, Protein 2 g, Fat 8 g, Carbohydrate 12 g, Fiber 4 g, Calcium 12 mg, Sodium 196 mg

1 Rinse the eggplant, leave unpeeled, and slice ½ inch thick. Cut the bell peppers into quarters, and remove the seeds.

2 Place the marinade ingredients in a blender, and process, or whip rapidly by hand to combine.

3 Place the sliced eggplant on a baking sheet, and brush with the marinade on both sides.

4 Preheat the grill, to high and allow to heat for about 5 minutes.

5 Place the eggplant on the hot grill; when dark grill marks appear, flip over and repeat.

You can also broil the eggplant in the oven. Set the oven to broil at 500°F. Place the baking pan with the eggplant on the top rack, and broil for about 12 minutes until the slices are medium brown. Remove and serve. If you cook them in the oven you only need to cook one side.

6 At the same time, grill the peppers skin side down until the skins are charred. Remove from the grill and cool, then peel off the skins.

7 For an appetizer salad, place the grilled eggplant overlapping on a bed of lettuce, and garnish with the roasted peppers.

GRILLED VEGETABLES

The barbecue grill plays a great role in our cuisine. It will truly liven up your meals. The vegetables below are excellent for grilling, but experiment with your favorites. For added flavor sensations, place some water-soaked mesquite or hickory chips over the grill stones before using.

Marinade

½ cup canola, peanut, or olive oil

1 tablespoon chopped fresh herbs (basil, oregano, tarragon, thyme, rosemary etc., or any combination of your favorite fresh herbs—dry herbs will do in a pinch)

1 teaspoon minced garlic

1 tablespoon Bragg Liquid Aminos

Dash of cayenne pepper

Eggplant, zucchini, summer squash, sweet or Idaho potatoes, green tomatoes, tomatillos, portobello or shiitake mushrooms, red, orange, or yellow bell peppers

1 Place all the marinade ingredients in a blender, and process, or whip rapidly by hand to combine.

2 Preheat the grill to high.

3 Rinse and slice your favorite vegetables ½ inch thick. If you are using peppers, clean and cut down the sides of the pepper so they lay flat. To grill mushrooms, destem and clean.

4 Arrange the vegetables on a baking pan, and brush lightly with the marinade.

5 Place the brushed side of the vegetables on the grill rack, and brush with more marinade while they are grilling.

6 When dark grill marks appear on the bottom, flip over the vegetables and repeat.

7 Serve hot, or if you would like the vegetables to be more tender, place in a 375°F oven to finish.

Orange and Ginger-glazed Plantains

Yield: 3 to 4 servings

Plantains, shaped like oversized bananas, are a mainstay of Caribbean cuisine. When yellow and firm, they are traditionally pan-fried, then mashed and refried. Hardly a low-fat preparation. Another way to enjoy plantains is to let them over-ripen, letting the skin turn black before using. This is how we will use them for this recipe.

1 cup freshly squeezed orange juice

⅔ cup brown rice syrup

1 tablespoon grated fresh ginger

2 very ripe plantains, peeled and cut in half lengthwise, then cut into quarters

2 teaspoons toasted sesame seeds

Per serving: Calories 352, Protein 2 g, Fat 0 g, Carbohydrate 83 g, Fiber 3 g, Calcium 31 mg, Sodium 8 mg

1 In a saucepan, combine the orange juice, syrup, and ginger. Bring to a rolling boil, and reduce to half of its original volume.

2 Preheat the oven to 400°F.

3 Place the sliced plantain flat side down in a casserole dish or on a baking sheet.

4 Drizzle the syrup over the plantains, then sprinkle on the sesame seeds.

5 Bake for 20 to 25 minutes until the syrup is a bubbly light brown but not burned. Serve hot with the remaining syrup.

Roasted Peppers

Roasting brings out the natural sweetness of bell peppers and imparts a slightly smoky taste. They are much easier to prepare than you think. We do not recommend using raw green bell peppers in our recipes due to the fact that they are an unripened pepper! However, roasted green peppers are acceptable. You may also try roasting the peppers skin side down on the grill or over an open flame while holding with them a pair of metal tongs until the skin is charred.

3 red, yellow, orange, or green bell peppers

1 teaspoon canola or peanut oil

Per serving: Calories 24, Protein 0 g, Fat 1 g, Carbohydrate 3 g, Fiber 1 g, Calcium 3 mg, Sodium 2 mg

1 Preheat the oven on the broil setting to 500°F.

2 Slice the peppers in a way that will allow the pepper to lie in flat, 2-inch wide slices.

3 Oil a baking pan lightly with a paper towel, and place the peppers skin side up on it.

4 Place the pan on the top rack of the preheated oven, and roast the peppers until they are slightly charred, approximately 15 to 20 minutes; remove.

5 Cover the pan with another inverted pan, and let the peppers steam for about 5 minutes. You may also place the peppers in a plastic bag, close it, and steam them for 5 minutes.

6 When cooled, remove the charred skin and serve the peppers either as is, julienned, or chopped as a garnish or complement to your favorite salads, vegetables, or entrees.

Spanakopitas

Yield: 8 to 10 servings

The classic Greek specialty is rekindled with soy mozzarella replacing the feta cheese. You may also add crumbled tofu.

Phyllo pastry is very delicate to work with. Its biggest enemies are air and water. When not using, be sure to keep covered with a towel or plastic wrap. Keep your work area dry. If the pastry tears or is broken, do not despair. Just patch it with more phyllo as necessary, but try to keep the top layer in one piece for a better presentation.

2 Vidalia or yellow onions, diced

2 teaspoons minced garlic

1 teaspoon canola or extra-virgin olive oil

2 pounds frozen chopped spinach, thawed and pressed dry in a strainer

Dash of cayenne pepper

½ teaspoon nutmeg

8 ounces soy mozzarella, shredded or cubed

¼ cup canola or peanut oil

One 12-ounce package phyllo pastry (see note above right)

Per serving: Calories 263, Protein 11 g, Fat 10 g, Carbohydrate 33 g, Fiber 7 g, Calcium 337 mg, Sodium 431 mg

1 Preheat the oven to 375°F.

2 Lightly brown the onions and garlic in the teaspoon of canola oil.

3 In a mixing bowl, toss the spinach, spices, and mozzarella together.

4 Brush the bottom of a 9 x 13-inch casserole lightly with the some of the remaining canola oil.

5 Layer 2 pieces of phyllo on the bottom of the pan, and brush lightly with oil. The pastry will be too large for the dish, but you may precut it to come up the sides of the pan.

6 Repeat step 5 with 2 more layers of pastry, and brush lightly with oil again.

7 Spread the spinach mixture evenly over the pastry, being sure to fill the corners.

8 At this point you can fold the excess phyllo back over the top of the spinach mix.

9 Cover the spinach with 2 more layers of phyllo, tucking it into the sides and corners of the pan with the pastry brush; brush lightly with oil.

10 Place on 2 more layers of pastry using the same procedures as above. For easier serving, pre-cut the pastry into squares before baking. Dip a pastry brush into water, and brush along the cut pastry lines. This will reduce some of the flakiness when serving. (A special thank you to Demetra Abdulla for this helpful hint.)

11 Bake on the top oven rack for 20 to 25 minutes, or until golden brown.

12 Remove from oven and serve with a sharp spatula. If you do not serve when hot, the phyllo may soften. Simply return the casserole to the oven, and reheat until crispy. If there are leftovers, remove from the refrigerator, bring to room temperature, and reheat at 375°F for 12 to 15 minutes until the pastry is crispy.

Summer Squash Sauté

Yield: 4 servings

This very colorful vegetable can be made fat-free by replacing the olive oil with vegetable broth.

1 Vidalia or yellow onion, peeled and cut in half

1 teaspoon minced garlic

4 yellow squash

1 red bell pepper

1 teaspoon extra-virgin olive oil

2 teaspoons chopped fresh oregano

Dash of cayenne pepper

Per serving: Calories 73, Protein 2 g, Fat 1 g, Carbohydrate 13 g, Fiber 4 g, Calcium 71 mg, Sodium 4 mg

1 Cut the onion into ¼-inch-thick slices. Slice the squash in half lengthwise, scoop out the seeds with a spoon, and slice ½ inch thick. Remove the seeds from the bell pepper, and cut into 1-inch cubes.

2 Heat the oil and lightly brown the onion and garlic.

3 Add the squash and peppers, cook on medium-high heat, and toss in the oregano and cayenne.

4 Adjust the spices to taste, and serve hot.

Tangy Carrots

Yield: 4 to 6 servings

If you are looking to liven up your steamed carrots, look no further than the recipe below. For additional variety you can try this recipe with julienned turnips, parsnips, jicama, fresh beets, or any combination of these vegetables.

6 carrots, scrubbed and diagonally
   sliced ¼ inch thick

½ cup brown rice syrup

⅓ cup freshly squeezed lime juice

2 teaspoons grated fresh ginger

Per serving: Calories 182, Protein 1 g,
Fat 0 g, Carbohydrate 45 g, Fiber 3 g,
Calcium 32 mg, Sodium 40 mg

1 Boil or steam the carrots 6 to 8 minutes until just tender.

2 Combine the rest of the ingredients in a blender.

3 Heat the sauce, add the carrots, toss, and serve hot.

Yuca Home Fries

Yield: 4 to 6 servings

Yuca is a wonderful root vegetable used mainly in Caribbean cooking. Long and tapered in shape with a dark husk, yuca is a nutritious vegetable that can be made in a variety of ways much like a potato.

It is quite often enjoyed in its simplest form: boiled until tender and tossed with fresh minced garlic, olive oil, salt, and pepper. Other Caribbean root vegetables, such as boniato and malanga, can be prepared the same way or even mashed like potatoes. Here is a way of enjoying yuca that our guests at the spa are just crazy about.

1½ pounds yuca

1 tablespoon coarsely chopped fresh cilantro

1 tablespoon lemon juice

¼ teaspoon sea salt, or 2 teaspoons yellow miso (optional)

Dash of cayenne pepper, or ⅛ teaspoon freshly ground pepper

2 tablespoons extra-virgin olive oil

Per serving: Calories 197, Protein 2 g, Fat 6 g, Carbohydrate 35 g, Fiber 3 g, Calcium 14 mg, Sodium 11 mg

1 Peel away the thick skin from the yuca until only the white flesh remains. If the yuca is very long, cut it into 3- to 4-inch cylinder-shaped pieces that are more manageable to work with.

2 Split the yuca lengthwise in half. Remove the small, fibrous piece that runs lengthwise down the center of the yuca by making a V-cut lengthwise along the center.

3 Split the yuca lengthwise again, and cut it into 1-inch cubes, much like a potato would be cut to make home fries. Rinse the yuca with some cool water before boiling.

4 Bring a pot of water to a boil, and cook the yuca about 12 to 15 minutes until it is tender, but not mushy. Pour the cooked yuca into a colander to drain.

5 While the yuca is cooking, preheat the oven to 425°F.

6 Process the remaining ingredients in a blender until creamy.

7 In a bowl large enough to accommodate mixing, toss the yuca and the cilantro sauce together. Place in a baking pan, and bake on the bottom oven rack about 25 minutes until lightly browned.

YUCA STEAK FRIES

When entertaining my friends, one of the most requested specialties of mine is yuca steak fries. To do this, cut the yuca into larger steak–fry sizes, and boil as below, being careful not to overcook. Now the nasty part: Turn on your deep fryer and fry the yuca until lightly browned and crispy. Remove and toss with sea salt, garlic powder, and pepper. Replace the olive oil in the sauce recipe with the same amount of mayonnaise alternative, and use this as a dipping sauce for the yuca fries.

DESSERTS

Almost Rum Balls

Yield: approximately 2 dozen

You will find this holiday dessert can be a wonderful "petit four" throughout the year.

1¼ cups whole almonds (Slices or slivers can be substituted if whole almonds are unavailable.)

½ cup raisins or pitted Medjoul dates

1 tablespoon carob powder

1 tablespoon vanilla extract

2 tablespoons brown rice syrup

Carob powder, coconut flakes, or crushed nuts, for coating

Per ball: Calories 62, Protein 1 g, Fat 4 g, Carbohydrate 5 g, Fiber 1 g, Calcium 23 mg, Sodium 2 mg

1 In a food processor, coarsely grind the almonds, then add and process the remaining ingredients.

2 Form the mixture into 1-inch balls, and roll with the palms of your hand. If you use your fingers too much, the balls will not be uniformly round.

3 Coat the balls with carob powder, coconut flakes, or crushed nuts, and serve.

APPLE-CHEESE CRISP

Yield: 6 to 8 servings

This warm dessert can be enjoyed by itself or over vanilla nondairy ice cream. For variety, try using pears or mangoes in place of the apples, or any combination of the three.

Apple Filling

6 red Delicious or Granny Smith apples

Juice of 2 lemons

¾ cup raisins

1 teaspoon ground cinnamon

2 tablespoons whole grain pastry flour

⅓ cup apple juice

Topping

⅓ cup rolled oats

¼ cup wheat germ

¼ cup whole grain pastry flour

½ cup chopped walnuts or pecans

2 ounces soy cheddar, shredded

⅓ cup soy margarine, melted

Per serving: Calories 321, Protein 6 g, Fat 15 g, Carbohydrate 40 g, Fiber 7 g, Calcium 86 mg, Sodium 169 mg

1 Peel and core the apples, and cut into ½-inch slices.

2 Toss the filling ingredients together, and place in a 9 x 12-inch casserole dish.

3 Preheat the oven to 375°F.

4 Spread the topping evenly over the apple filling, and bake on the top oven rack for 25 to 30 minutes, or until browned and crispy.

Apple-Pear Phyllo Tarts

Yield: 6 to 8 tarts

Your guests will always remember what they ate last at a dinner party. They will not forget this crispy, low–fat tart. For an added touch, line an entree plate with Tofu Sabayon Sauce, page 229, and place the tart in the center.

2 Anjou pears

2 Granny Smith apples

2 tablespoons fresh lemon juice

2 teaspoons ground cinnamon

½ teaspoon ground nutmeg

⅓ cup raisins

½ cup toasted almond slices or slivers

One 12-ounce box phyllo dough

2 tablespoons canola oil

Per tart: Calories 224, Protein 3 g, Fat 8 g, Carbohydrate 33 g, Fiber 5 g, Calcium 38 mg, Sodium 79 mg

1 Peel and core the pears and apples, and cut into ½-inch slices.

2 Preheat the oven to 375°F.

3 Combine the pears, apples, lemon juice, cinnamon, nutmeg, and raisins in a large mixing bowl.

4 Place the mixture in a saucepan, cover, and simmer for 10 minutes until the fruit is just tender.

5 Set the mix aside and fold in the toasted almonds.

6 Open the phyllo and lay out the first 2 sheets on a clean, dry table, being careful to keep the remaining sheets covered so they won't dry out.

7 With a pastry brush, lightly brush the phyllo with a little of the canola oil.

8 Lay 2 more sheets of pastry over the first 2, and brush with oil again.

9 Repeat again with 2 more layers of pastry, and brush with oil again.

10 Lightly rub the tins of a large muffin pan with canola oil.

11 Cut the phyllo in 6 to 8s even squares, and form a cup inside each muffin tin. Overlap the parts of the pastry that fall outside the muffin tins. Repeat again for more tarts.

12 Spoon the fruit mixture into the phyllo cups to about ⅔ full. Fold over the outside pastry to enclose the tart. It does not have to be perfect.

13 Sprinkle the tops with ground cinnamon, and bake for 18 to 20 minutes, or until the tops of the tarts are brown and crispy.

14 Remove the tarts from the oven, and let cool for a couple of minutes. Remove from the tins carefully with a rubber spatula, and serve.

Banana Cream Pie

Yield: 8 servings

Made from only frozen bananas, this is a delicious dessert. We use this pie to celebrate birthdays and other special occasions. There are two different ways to prepare the filling. A Champion juicer with the ice cream attachment will provide the best results, making a filling that will be ready to serve quickly.

You can garnish the top of the pie by spreading tofu whip cream and freezing again before cutting. Also try folding ground cinnamon, chopped nuts, coconut flakes, or carob chips into the filling before filling the pie shell.

Pie Crust (makes 2)

1¼ cups whole almonds (Slices or slivers can be substituted if whole are unavailable.)

⅔ cup raisins

1 tablespoon carob powder

1 teaspoon vanilla extract

2 tablespoons brown rice syrup

8 ripe bananas, peeled

½ cup apple juice (for processor or blender method only)

1 In a food processor, coarsely grind the almonds, then add the remaining crust ingredients and pulse until well blended.

2 Press the crust mixture into the bottom and up the sides of a 9-inch pie plate. Save the remaining crust mixture for later use.

Champion Juicer Method

1 When the bananas have become very ripe, peel and freeze them for 8 hours or more.

2 Install the ice cream dispenser parts of the juicer, and push the frozen fruit through the chamber.

3 After all the fruit has been processed, spread evenly into the pie shell.

4 Return the pie to the freezer for a minimum of 2 hours. Cut and serve.

Food Processor or Blender Method

1 Cut the bananas into chunks.

2 Place the bananas and juice in a food processor, and process until well blended.

3 Pour into the pie shell, and freeze 4 to 6 hours, or until firm.

4 Remove the pie from the freezer about 30 minutes before cutting. Garnish, cut, and serve.

Berry-Mango Phyllo Strudel

Yield: 1 roll (4 to 6 servings)

This is an exciting but light alternative to the traditional puff pastry strudels! Tofu Sabayon Sauce, page 229, will provide a delicious touch of vanilla to this strudel.

2 ripe mangoes, peeled, seeded, and cut into ½-inch cubes

1 pint raspberries, blackberries, blueberries, or quartered strawberries

2 tablespoons brown rice syrup (optional—if the berries are too sour for you)

2 teaspoons ground cinnamon, with additional for topping

One 12-ounce box phyllo pastry

2 tablespoons canola oil

Per serving: Calories 271, Protein 4 g, Fat 5 g, Carbohydrate 50 g, Fiber 6 g, Calcium 18 mg, Sodium 182 mg

1 Preheat the oven to 375°F.

2 Lightly toss the mangoes, berries, syrup, and cinnamon in a bowl, and set aside.

3 Open the phyllo and lay out the first 2 sheets on a clean, dry table.

4 With a pastry brush, lightly brush the phyllo with the canola oil.

5 Lay 2 more sheets of phyllo over the first 2, and brush with oil again.

6 Repeat again with 2 more layers of pastry, and brush with oil.

7 Place the fruit mixture evenly across one side of the pastry, and roll the pastry over the fruit as if making a jelly roll. Tuck the ends of the pastry under the roll.

8 Place the rolled pastry on a baking sheet, brush lightly with oil, and dust with additional cinnamon. With the tip of a knife, cut a few air vents in the top of the pastry. Brush all over lightly with cool water.

9 Bake 20 to 25 minutes until golden brown. Remove from the oven and let cool.

10 Slice on an angle with a sharp knife, and serve warm.

BURGUNDY POACHED PEARS

Yield: 4 servings

We celebrated Valentine's Day with this ruby colored dessert. You may also try Granny Smith apples in place of the pears.

1 bottle (750 ml) nonalcoholic dry red, full-bodied wine, such as Burgundy-style

4 Anjou pears

2 tablespoons fresh lemon juice

4 cinnamon sticks

½ cup raisins

2 tablespoons Sucanat

2 tablespoons arrowroot

¼ cup water

Per serving: Calories 254, Protein 2 g, Fat 0 g, Carbohydrate 60 g, Fiber 6 g, Calcium 42 mg, Sodium 29 mg

1 Bring the wine to a boil in a deep saucepan.

2 Peel and core the pears, and toss with the the lemon juice to prevent discoloring.

3 Place the cinnamon sticks and pears in the wine, cover, and cook for about 20 minutes until the pears are tender. Be careful not to overcook.

4 Remove the pears with a slotted spoon, and refrigerate. Reserve the cooking liquid.

5 While the wine is still hot, pour it over the raisins, and allow them to plump while the pears are cooling.

6 Strain the plumped raisins, reserving the wine. Stuff the raisins inside the pears and refrigerate.

7 Place 1 cup of the strained wine in a saucepan, and heat to a boil. Sprinkle the Sucanat into the wine. Dissolve the arrowroot in the water, and whip into the simmering wine until thickened. If the sauce becomes too thick, thin it with some more of the wine.

8 Line an entree plate with the wine sauce, and place the chilled pear in the center of the plate.

9 To garnish, insert the cooked cinnamon stick in the top of the pear to serve as the stem. Raspberries, blackberries, or peppermint leaves can be used as a garnish.

CAPPUCCINO MOUSSE WITH CAROB CHIPS

Yield: 3 to 4 servings

This is a caffeine–free pudding that has our guests begging for more and wondering how in the heck did we do that. Here is the mystery recipe. Serve with a tofu whip cream garnish and a sprinkle of carob powder or carob chips.

One 12.3-ounce box extra-firm silken tofu

2 tablespoons carob or vanilla soymilk

3 tablespoons Sucanat

1 teaspoon vanilla extract

2 tablespoons instant coffee alternative

⅓ cup carob chips

1 Purée everything, except the carob chips, in a blender or food processor until creamy.

2 Fold in the carob chips, and refrigerate until cool before serving.

Per serving: Calories 147, Protein 8 g, Fat 5 g, Carbohydrate 18 g, Fiber 2 g, Calcium 60 mg, Sodium 36 mg

Key Lime Cheesecake

Yield: 8 servings (one 9-inch pie)

You will not believe how incredibly delicious this is. It tastes like the real thing, only better. You can replace the lime juice and zest with lemon to get a more traditional cheesecake flavor.

Graham Cracker Crust

½ cup chopped almonds

1 cup whole wheat graham cracker crumbs

3 tablespoons Sucanat

3 tablespoons non-hydrogenated vegan margarine (such as Earth Balance)

Filling

One 12.3-ounce box extra-firm silken tofu

8 ounces plain soy cream cheese

1 cup non-dairy sour cream

½ cup Sucanat

⅓ cup lime juice

2 teaspoons lime zest

1 teaspoon vanilla extract

Per serving: Calories 387, Protein 7 g, Fat 24 g, Carbohydrate 29 g, Fiber 2 g, Calcium 66 mg, Sodium 320 mg

1 Toast the almonds in a heavy skillet for about 10 minutes until lightly brown.

2 To make the crust, combine the almonds, graham cracker crumbs, and Sucanat in a medium bowl. Melt the margarine in a small pan, pour over the dry crust ingredients, and combine.

3 Spray a 9-inch pie pan with canola oil. Press the crust into the bottom and sides of the pan, and refrigerate for about 30 minutes.

4 Preheat the oven to 300°F. Purée the filling ingredients in a food processor until very creamy, stopping several times to scrape down the inside of the processor bowl.

5 Pour the filling into the pie crust, and bake on the middle oven rack for about 40 minutes. Placing the filled pie in a large baking pan with ½ inch of water will help ensure even baking and keep the pie from cracking as it bakes.

6 Allow the pie to cool on a wire rack or refrigerator shelf. Do not serve until chilled thoroughly.

Vegetable sushi rolls, p. 150–52.

Dessert Fruit Sauce

Yield: 1⅓ cups

A colorful pool of fruit sauce on the bottom of a dessert plate truly adds to the presentation. All you need is a blender and a squeeze bottle to do what chefs have done for years in the finest restaurants. This sauce will keep in the refrigerator for 1 week or more. You may also try other ripe fruits such as peeled mangoes, papaya, peaches, or raspberries.

1 cup fresh strawberries or kiwi,
    peeled and quartered

⅓ cup brown rice syrup

Per ¼ cup: Calories 74, Protein 0 g,
Fat 0 g, Carbohydrate 18 g, Fiber 1 g,
Calcium 5 mg, Sodium 1 mg

1 Place the ingredients in a blender, and purée until well blended.

2 Pour the sauce onto the center of an dessert plate, and tilt the plate from side to side to coat evenly. You may also elect to pour the sauce into a squeeze bottle and squirt around the border of your dessert plate to decorate. Place your dessert in the center of the plate.

Raspberry–Mango Strudel, pp. 220–21

Luscious Lemon Pie

Yield: 8 servings

With the assistance of my friend, vegetarian Chef Ken Hubscher, this recipe was created.

½ cup toasted sesame seeds

1½ cups oat flour (process rolled oats in a blender)

¼ cup canola oil

¼ cup brown rice syrup

2 teaspoons vanilla extract

¼ teaspoon sea salt

Pie Filling

1 cup apple juice

2 tablespoons agar powder

¾ cup brown rice syrup

Pinch of sea salt

½ cup fresh lemon juice (Grate 1 teaspoon of the zest and set aside before juicing.)

1 teaspoon vanilla extract

2 tablespoons arrowroot combined with ¼ cup apple juice until dissolved

1 cup Tofu Whipped Cream, page 230 (optional)

¼ cup toasted coconut flakes (optional)

Directions for Crust

1 Preheat the oven to 375°F.

2 Toast the sesame seeds about 18 minutes or until brown.

3 Mix the oat flour and toasted sesame seeds in a large bowl.

4 In a separate bowl, whip together the remaining ingredients.

5 Combine the wet mix with the dry, being careful not to over-mix.

6 Press the dough evenly about ⅛ inch thick onto the bottom and sides of a pie shell.

7 Bake for about 20 minutes or until the crust is brown. Cool the pie crust in the refrigerator. While the pie crust is baking, begin the preparation of the pie filling.

Directions for Filling

1 Combine the 1 cup apple juice and agar in a blender. Transfer the mixture to a pot, cover, and let rest for 15 minutes, stirring occasionally to dissolve.

2 Slowly heat the juice mixture over low heat for about 5 to 10 minutes, stirring frequently until dissolved. Keep the mixture covered to avoid forming a skin.

3 When the agar is dissolved, add the brown rice syrup, salt, and lemon juice, lemon zest, and vanilla.

4 Bring the agar mixture to a boil, whip in the arrowroot mixture, and simmer until it is clear and dissolved.

5 Pour the mixture into the baked pie crust, and refrigerate 3 to 4 hours until the filling is set.

6 Remove the pie and spread a ½-inch layer of Tofu Whipped Cream over the top, if desired.

7 Dust with the toasted coconut flakes, and garnish each serving with a half lemon slice.

Per serving: Calories 337, Protein 4 g, Fat 11 g, Carbohydrate 53 g, Fiber 3 g, Calcium 108 mg, Sodium 71 mg

PUMPKIN PIE

Yield: 2 pies (16 servings)

This is a nondairy version of an American favorite. We use sweet potatoes to compensate for the omission of eggs in this recipe.

2 whole wheat or rice pie crusts

One 28-ounce can pumpkin purée

1 large baked sweet potato, peeled and mashed

½ cup maple syrup

⅔ cup vanilla soymilk

2 tablespoons Ener-G egg replacer powder

1½ teaspoons ground cinnamon

½ teaspoon nutmeg

1 teaspoon vanilla extract

Per serving: Calories 180, Protein 3 g, Fat 7 g, Carbohydrate 25 g, Fiber 4 g, Calcium 33 mg, Sodium 84 mg

1 Preheat the oven to 400°F, and bake the pie crusts for 12 minutes.

2 Thoroughly combine the pumpkin, sweet potato, and maple syrup ina food processor.

3 Blend the soymilk with the remaining ingredients.

4 Combine the soymilk mixture with the pumpkin mixture, and stir.

5 Pour the mixture into the pie shells, and bake at 325°F for 40 minutes. Refrigerate the pies until well chilled.

6 Cut each pie into 8 pieces, garnish with Tofu Whipped Cream, page 230, and serve.

Tofu Sabayon Sauce

Yield: approximately 2 cups

This low-fat, cholesterol-free version of the French vanilla dessert sauce (or, as the Italians call it, zabaglione) is easy to prepare. Just thinking about the days of using heavy cream and egg yolks to prepare this sauce makes me cringe! This recipe sure gives me a lot of peace of mind when serving it. It can also be used as a tasty and colorful sauce base below a fruit phyllo strudel or tart.

One 12.3-ounce box low-fat firm or extra-firm silken tofu

¾ cup soymilk, almond milk, or rice milk

Pinch of saffron threads or turmeric

½ cup brown rice or maple syrup

2 teaspoons vanilla extract

Per ¼ cup: Calories 73, Protein 1 g, Fat 0 g, Carbohydrate 16 g, Fiber 0 g, Calcium 2 mg, Sodium 4 mg

1 Drain and blot the tofu dry with paper towels, and break into chunks.

2 Place the tofu in a blender with all the other ingredients, and purée until smooth. Adjust the consistency of the sauce using tofu to thicken it or soymilk to thin it.

Tofu Whipped Cream

Yield: 2 cups (4 servings)

You will be pleasantly surprised with the flavor and fluffiness of this nutritious version of whipped cream. For a thicker cream, add more tofu—for a thinner cream, add more lemon juice. Many thanks to Gloria Wilburn for providing this recipe.

One 12.3-ounce box low-fat extra-firm silken tofu

1 tablespoon canola oil

3 tablespoons maple or brown rice syrup, or 2 tablespoons Sucanat

1 tablespoon fresh lemon juice

2 teaspoons vanilla extract

Per serving: Calories 116, Protein 6 g, Fat 4 g, Carbohydrate 13 g, Fiber 0 g, Calcium 1 mg, Sodium 83 mg

1 Drain and blot the tofu dry with paper towels.

2 Break the tofu into cubes, place in a blender with all the ingredients, and whip until fluffy. Turn the blender off and scrape down the sides to be sure no tofu chunks are remaining, and purée until smooth.

Chocolate Tofu Mousse

Yield: 4 servings

You can also use 1 cup of strawberries or kiwis in place of the cocoa for a fruit mousse.

2 cups Tofu Whipped Cream (above)

2 tablespoons low-fat cocoa powder or carob powder

Per serving: Calories 127, Protein 7 g, Fat 4 g, Carbohydrate 15 g, Fiber 1 g, Calcium 5 mg, Sodium 84 mg

1 Place the ingredients in a blender, and process until smooth. Serve well chilled.

VERY VANILLA CAKE

Yield: 8 to 10 servings

This easy-to-prepare cake can be made lighter by using water or rice milk in place of the soymilk. The vinegar used here reacts with the baking soda to enhance its leavening action.

1¾ cups whole grain pastry flour

1 teaspoon baking powder

1 teaspoon baking soda

½ teaspoon sea salt

¾ cup brown rice syrup or maple syrup

⅔ cup soymilk, rice milk, or pure or distilled water

⅓ cup canola oil

2 tablespoons vanilla extract

1 tablespoon apple cider vinegar

Per serving: Calories 237, Protein 3 g, Fat 9 g, Carbohydrate 38 g, Fiber 3 g, Calcium 7 mg, Sodium 124 mg

1 Preheat the oven to 350°F.

2 In a mixing bowl, combine the flour, baking powder, baking soda, and salt.

3 In a separate bowl, whip together the remaining ingredients.

4 Add the wet mix to the dry mix, and blend together until smooth.

5 Oil an 8-inch cake pan with canola oil, and pour in the batter.

6 Bake for 35 to 40 minutes, or until the center is firm to the touch.

7 Cool at room temperature before cutting. Serve with Tofu Whipped Cream, page 230, as a garnish.

Carob Chip Cookies

Yield: approximately 24 cookies

These cookies are scrumptious. They can be flavored with coconut or chopped nuts.

Liquid ingredients

¼ cup canola oil

¾ cup brown rice syrup

3 tablespoons pure or distilled water

1 tablespoon vanilla extract

1 tablespoon Ener-G egg replacer powder

1 cup whole wheat flour

1 cup wheat germ

½ teaspoon powdered ginger (optional)

1 cup unsweetened carob chips

½ cup chopped walnuts, pecans, or macadamia nuts (optional)

½ cup unsweetened unrefined coconut flakes (optional)

Per cookie: Calories 109, Protein 3 g, Fat 4 g, Carbohydrate 16 g, Fiber 1 g, Calcium 17 mg, Sodium 5 mg

1 Whip together the liquid ingredients and egg replacer until smooth.

2 Blend in the flour, wheat germ, and ginger.

3 Fold in the carob chips and nuts or coconut until well blended.

4 Preheat the oven to 325°F.

5 Spoon the cookies onto an oiled baking sheet 1 inch apart.

6 Bake for 15 to 18 minutes until golden brown.

Oatmeal Raisin Cookies

Yield: approximately 18 cookies

We can never make enough of these scrumptious cookies for our guests at the Spa.

¼ cup canola oil

¾ cup brown rice syrup

3 tablespoons distilled or pure water

1 tablespoon Ener-G egg replacer powder

1 tablespoon vanilla extract

1 cup whole wheat pastry flour

1 cup rolled oats

1 teaspoon cinnamon

1 cup raisins, softened in warm water and drained

½ cup unsweetened coconut flakes (optional)

Per cookie: Calories 137, Protein 2 g, Fat 3 g, Carbohydrate 24 g, Fiber 2 g, Calcium 8 mg, Sodium 8 mg

1 Preheat the oven to 325°F.

2 Whip together the canola oil, brown rice syrup, water, egg replacer, and vanilla until smooth.

3 Blend in the flour, oatmeal, and cinnamon.

4 Fold in the raisins and coconut until well blended.

5 Spoon the cookies onto an oiled cookie sheet about 1 inch apart.

6 Bake for 15 to 18 minutes until golden brown.

Peanut Butter Cookies

Yield: approximately 18 cookies

If you are still a "cookie monster," these cookies are definitely for you.

¾ cup low-sodium peanut butter

½ cup barley malt syrup

¼ cup canola oil

2 tablespoons vanilla soymilk

2 teaspoons vanilla extract

½ cup Sucanat

1 cup rolled oats

¾ cup whole grain pastry flour

2 teaspoons baking powder

½ cup unsalted roasted peanuts

½ cup carob chips (optional)

Per cookie: Calories 198, Protein 5 g,
Fat 10 g, Carbohydrate 22 g, Fiber 2 g,
Calcium 12 mg, Sodium 4 mg

1 Preheat the oven to 325°F. Blend together the peanut butter, barley malt syrup, canola oil, soymilk, and vanilla in a large mixing bowl.

2 Combine the Sucanat, rolled oats, wheat flour, and baking powder in another bowl.

3 Fold the dry mixture into the peanut butter mixture, add the peanuts and carob chips, if desired, and mix well.

4 Spoon the dough onto an oiled cookie sheet, and flatten slightly with the back of a spoon or fork.

5 Bake for 15 to 18 minutes, and allow to cool before serving.

PUMPKIN CRANBERRY COOKIES

Yield: approximately 2 dozen cookies

This recipe is a modified version of one created by my good friend, Chef Steve Petusevsky, who writes for Cooking Light magazine. The ingredients below may seem lengthy, but the results are scrumptious. You can also substitute golden raisins for the cranberries here.

¼ cup low-sodium peanut butter

¼ cup soy margarine (non-hydrogenated if available)

½ cup Sucanat

½ cup maple syrup

2 teaspoons baking powder

½ teaspoon sea salt

½ teaspoon ground cinnamon

Dash of nutmeg

1 tablespoon Ener-G egg replacer powder

2 tablespoons pure or distilled water

1 cup pumpkin purée

2 cups whole grain pastry flour

½ cup rolled oats

1 cup sun-dried cranberries

Per cookie: Calories 114, Protein 2 g, Fat 3 g, Carbohydrate 18 g, Fiber 2 g, Calcium 16 mg, Sodium 72 mg

1 Preheat the oven to 375°F. Lightly oil a cookie sheet.

2 Blend the peanut butter and margarine until creamy.

3 Add the Sucanat, maple syrup, baking powder, salt, cinnamon, and nutmeg, and fold in thoroughly.

4 Mix together the egg replacer, water, and pumpkin purée, and add.

5 Fold in the flour, oats, and cranberries.

6 Spoon the mixture onto the cookie sheet about the size of silver dollars.

7 Bake for 15 to 20 minutes. Allow to cool before serving

Three-seed Banana Cookies

Yield: approximately 24 cookies

This is a wheat–free cookie that will keep you coming back for more! For added variety, you may try adding oatmeal, almond slivers, or any variety of chopped nuts.

8 to 10 ripe bananas, peeled and mashed

1 cup unsweetened coconut flakes

1 cup raisins

½ cup hulled sesame seeds

¼ cup flaxseeds

¼ cup hulled sunflower seeds

Per cookie: Calories 154, Protein 2 g, Fat 9 g, Carbohydrate 17 g, Fiber 3 g, Calcium 44 mg, Sodium 6 mg

1 This recipe can be baked in a dehydrator or in an oven. Turn on the dehydrator or preheat the oven to 225°F.

2 In a large bowl, mash the bananas thoroughly.

3 Add the remaining ingredients, and mix thoroughly.

4 With a teaspoon, scoop and form the cookies, and place on the dehydrator racks or on a lightly oiled cookie sheet.

5 If using a dehydrator, bake for 2 days, or until the cookies are crispy. If using an oven, bake for 6 to 8 hours, or until crispy and lightly browned. We usually place them in the oven before going to bed. It makes for a nice morning surprise!

To save time and the labor of scooping the cookies, simply spoon this mixture into an 10 x 13 oiled casserole dish or cookie sheet to bake them and cut them into squares a la brownies.

JUICE FASTING

JUICE FAST

Recipes and Schedule

I receive many requests for the juice fast recipes we use at the spa. Ideally, an extended juice fast should be supervised by an expert on fasting. However, you may try a three-day fast as a way of cleansing the body. The amount of juice to drink per meal is 16 to 20 ounces. Any more juice than that is difficult for the stomach to handle.

Juice fasts are not a permanent solution to weight loss. They may be beneficial to "jump start" a weight-loss program. Fasting is also a way of reducing cravings for salt, sugar, and sweets. Always strain your juices during a fast. If it is a strict fast, do not eat any whole foods at all. The idea is to remove the fiber from your diet temporarily. This is also one way of avoiding hunger during your fast.

One of the positives of juice fasting versus the more demanding water fast program is that you can maintain your normal daily activities and exercise programs without feeling rundown. You should actually be feeling great during your fast.

Feel free to drink plenty of water or sodium-free vegetable broth in between your juices. Try the recipe in this book for Vegetable Broth, page 91, (the "Potassium Broth" we use at the Regency).

After a fast, it is a good idea to "break the fast" by starting with fresh melons for your first meal, then move on to salads, then cooked foods. If you jump right back into heavier foods, you may experience some stomach pains.

I also like to use fresh vegetable juices between meals or before or after a workout for that nutrient energy boost. I find it also helps to relieve some of my sweet tooth cravings during the day.

Be sure to drink your juice within 15 minutes or sooner after making it. After 1 hour, the living enzymes begin to break down, and by the next day they are gone. If vegetable juices sit too long, they may become bitter and lose flavor.

If for whatever reason you feel light-headed or experience other discomforts during your fast, cut back on your activities, stop your fast, and call your nutritionist.

You will need a juice-extracting machine. Champion makes a good one that also doubles as an ice cream and nut butter maker. There are other good machines out there that can be found in most department stores.

To save time, you can also clean your vegetables in advance, up to 3 days, and store them refrigerated in a plastic bag to retain their freshness.

You may choose a 3-drink fast or a 5-drink fast depending on how you feel the first day, or from your past experiences.

BREAKFAST JUICE

16 ounces

Freshly squeezed orange juice, grapefruit juice, or a combination of the two.

You may hand squeeze the juice or peel away the outer rind and put it through your juice extractor

Per serving (juices): Calories 221, Protein 3 g, Fat 0 g, Carbohydrate 51 g, Fiber 0 g, Calcium 53 mg, Sodium 5 mg

or

16 ounces fruit smoothie

1 pint strawberries, rinsed, stems remove

1 papaya, peeled and seeded

½ golden pineapple (they are the sweetest), peeled and cut in half, core trimmed (Save the other half for the next day.)

Push the fruit through your juicer, and strain if necessary. You may also replace the strawberries with blueberries, cranberries, or grapes.

Per smoothie: Calories 361, Protein 4 g, Fat 2 g, Carbohydrate 80 g, Fiber 0 g, Calcium 136 mg, Sodium 14 mg

MID-MORNING JUICE

16 ounces vegetable juice

- 4 romaine or kale leaves, or 2 ounces spinach leaves
- 4 organic carrots, scrubbed (Cut off both ends and save for vegetable broth.)
- 4 celery stalks, rinsed well (Cut away leaves and bottoms, and save for vegetable broth.)
- 1 apple, cut in quarters

Per serving: Calories 263, Protein 5 g, Fat 0 g, Carbohydrate 58 g, Fiber 0 g, Calcium 234 mg, Sodium 271 mg

LUNCH JUICE

16 ounces

Fresh watermelon juice, or an orange and grapefruit juice combo

Peel away the rind of the watermelon, leaving a little of the white pulp intact—there is valuable nutrition stored in the white pulp.

Per serving: Calories 142, Protein 2 g, Fat 1 g, Carbohydrate 29 g, Fiber 0 g, Calcium 37 mg, Sodium 9 mg

MID-AFTERNOON JUICE

16 ounces green juice

- 6 romaine or kale leaves, or 2 ounces spinach leaves
- 6 celery stalks, rinsed well
- 1 to 2 apples, quartered

Per serving: Calories 170, Protein 1 g, Fat 0 g, Carbohydrate 38 g, Fiber 0 g, Calcium 145 mg, Sodium 220 mg

EVENING DINNER JUICE

16 ounces vegetable juice

4 romaine or kale leaves, or 2 ounces spinach leaves

4 organic carrots, scrubbed

4 celery stalks, rinsed well

1 apple

Trim away the leaves and ends of the carrots and celery as for mid-morning juice.

You may also choose to add other personal touches to your juice. Try a small piece of peeled fresh ginger or garlic clove (if you will not be around others!) A vine-ripe tomato or a wedge of fresh red beet can be added to your vegetable juice.

Per serving: Calories 237, Protein 3 g, Fat 0 g, Carbohydrate 53 g, Fiber 0 g, Calcium 170 mg, Sodium 245 mg

Remember to drink your juice slowly—with a straw if that helps make it more of an event. If you drink it too quickly, you may have felt like you missed your meal and not given yourself time to enjoy the flavors.

By the end of the first day, you should have saved enough carrot and celery ends and pieces to begin a vegetable broth stock pot the next day (see recipe, page 91).

SAMPLE MENUS To assist with a well rounded meal program, we have listed a typical lunch menu and 4 weeks of dinner menus.

LUNCH MENU

Sunday
Garden salad with Mustard Tahini Dressing, p. 48

Broccoli and Cheddar Quiche, p. 124

Monday
Tossed salad with Low-Fat Dressings, pp. 44-54

Cream of Broccoli Soup, p. 74

Tuesday
Vegetarian Roulade with Hummus, p. 102, and Tahini Dressing, p. 54

Wednesday
Garden salad with Creamy Garlic Dressing, p. 46

Greek Pasta Salad, p. 36

Thursday
Waldorf Salad, p. 33, on a bed of romaine lettuce

Banana Cream Pie, p. 218

Friday
Green leaf salad with assorted sprouts and nuts

Tahini Dressing, p. 54, with fresh basil

Saturday
Caesar Salad, p. 29, with Pita Croutons, p. 96, and baked Italian tofu slices (store bought),

Baked Potato, p. 182, with stone-ground mustard or baked sweet potato

DINNER MENU - WEEK 1

Sunday
Tofu Terrine with Sun-Dried Tomatoes and Pesto, p. 140

Angel Hair Pasta Pomodori Salad, p. 24

Monday
Garden salad with Sweet and Spicy Mustard Dressing, p. 51

Risotto with Wild Mushrooms, p. 171

Steamed asparagus

Tuesday
Tossed salad with Creamy French Dressing, p. 46

Three Bean Enchiladas with Mexican Salsa, p. 62, and guacamole, pp. 130-31

Wednesday
Tossed salad with Peanut Butter Dressing, p. 50

"'Not So Sloppy Joes," p. 97, on whole wheat pita

Thursday
Caesar Salad, p. 29, with Pita Croutons, p. 96

Whole wheat angel hair pasta with Tofu Meatballs, p. 135, and Marinara Sauce, p. 61

Friday
Minestrone Soup, p. 84

Vegetable Pita Pizza, p. 180

Saturday
Gazpacho, p. 79

Oven-Fried Sweet Potato Spears, p. 190

Summer Squash Sauté p. 208

Steamed green beans

DINNER MENU - WEEK 2

Sunday
Vegetable Sushi Roll, pp. 150-52
Seaweed Cole Slaw, p. 38
Steamed or stir-fried vegetables
Grilled Tofu Steaks, p. 133

Monday
White and Black Bean Soup (Black Bean, p. 73, and Navy Bean, p. 89)
Garden salad with Tarragon Vinaigrette, p. 53
Whole wheat fettuccine with Marinara Sauce, p. 61
Swiss chard

Tuesday
Island Gumbo Soup, p. 80
Baked Potato Skins, p. 183, with soy cheddar cheese, soy sour cream, and fresh vegetable medley

Wednesday
Field greens with Raspberry-Tahini Dressing, p. 52
Savory Lentil Loaf, p. 172, with Grilled Vegetables, p. 203

Thursday
Fat-Free Cucumber-Dill Salad, p. 32
Black Beans and Corn Quesadillas, p. 154, with Mexican Salsa, p. 62, and guacamole

Friday
Spinach salad with Pineapple-Mustard Dressing, p. 51
Spinach Lasagne with Grilled Vegetables, pp. 116-17, and steamed sugar snap peas

Saturday
Spring Vegetable Soup, p. 90
Tossed salad with Balsamic Vinaigrette, p. 45
Vegetable Pita Pizza, p. 180

DINNER MENU - WEEK 3

Sunday
Asparagus and Shiitake Mushroom Salad, p. 25
Pad Thai-Style Noodles with Peanut Sauce, p. 112

Monday
Tossed salad with Apple-Mustard Dressing, p. 44
Eggplant Parmesan, pp. 126-27
Broccoli Rabe, p. 199

Tuesday
Lima Bean Soup, p. 81
Vegetable Pita Pizza, p. 180

Wednesday
Caesar Salad, p. 29, with baked Italian-style tofu (store-bought)
Twice-Stuffed Baked Potato, p. 191
Creamy Cauliflower and Baby Peas, p. 201

Thursday
Eggplant Napoleon, pp. 18-19
Chicken Seitan Stroganoff, p. 155, over brown rice

Friday
Garden salad with Balsamic Vinaigrette, p. 45
Sicilian-Style Orzo with Mushrooms, Olives, and Sun-Dried Tomatoes, p. 115

Saturday
Arugula salad with red onions and cucumbers
Citrus-Poppy Seed Dressing, p. 44
Tofu Eggplant Torte, pp. 138-39
Steamed asparagus

DINNER MENU - WEEK 4

Sunday
Vine-Ripe Tomatoes and Soy Mozzarella
with Pesto Sauce, p. 22

Kale and Mushroom Casserole, p. 166

Steamed sugar snap peas

Tangy Carrots, p. 209

Monday
Tossed salad with Mustard-Tahini Dressing,
p. 48

Vegetable Chili, pp. 178-79, over steamed
brown rice or quinoa

Tuesday
Miso Soup, p. 85

Tossed salad with Fat-Free Italian Dressing,
p. 47

Grilled Tofu Steaks, p. 133

Steamed Broccoli with Garlic, Tamari and
Coconut Sauce, p. 200

Wednesday
Tossed salad with Creamy Garlic Dressing,
p. 46

Penne Pasta with Sun-Dried Tomatoes,
Mushrooms and Pesto, p. 114

Steamed baby vegetables

Thursday
Vegan burger on a multi-grain roll, with
alfalfa sprouts, lettuce and tomato

Corn on the cob

Friday
Mesclun lettuce salad with Creamy French
Dressing, p. 46

Grilled Vegetable Burritos, pp. 162-63, with
Mexican Salsa, p. 62

Refried Beans, p. 170

Saturday
Hearts of Palm and Artichoke Salad, p. 37

Eggplant Rollatini with Marinara Sauce,
pp. 128-29

Spinach with roasted pine nuts and garlic

GLOSSARY

Agar—A sea vegetable that can be used as a vegan substitute for gelatin, an animal product. Agar is used mainly as a thickener for fruit jellies, pies, and aspic molds. It is rich in calcium, iron, vitamins A, B-complex, C, D, and iodine. Because it adds bulk to any meal without adding calories, agar is helpful in curbing appetite when dieting.

Arame—A mildly flavored sea vegetable that is very easy to use. It is shaped in short, dark strands, can be softened in warm water, and be ready to use in minutes. Because it is delicate, be careful not to oversoak or overhandle it as arame will fall apart very easily.

Arrowroot—A powdered flour from the root of the tropical arrowroot plant. It can be used in cooking to replace cornstarch, which is chemically processed. Arrowroot remains clear when added to thicken a sauce and is easily digested. Be sure to dissolve it first in cold water.

Balsamic vinegar—An Italian vinegar made from fermented grapes. Not as sour as traditional vinegars, balsamic actually tends to be almost sweet. The longer the balsamic is aged (sometimes as long as 80 years), the richer and sweeter the flavor will be.

Barley malt syrup—A natural sweetener made from sprouted whole barley. It has a caramel flavor and color. Compared to molasses, honey, or maple syrups, barley malt syrup has 75% less natural sugars.

Bok choy—A Chinese white cabbage with thick white stems and chard-like leaves. Often used in stir-fry dishes and Oriental salads.

Bouquet garni—A bunch of herbs tied together, usually in cheesecloth, and added to soups or sauces as they cook. It usually includes a bay leaf, thyme, peppercorns, parsley, and whatever herbs you may desire.

Bragg Liquid Aminos—A low-sodium non-fermented replacement for soy sauce or tamari. Bragg has about 25% less sodium than low-sodium soy sauce products.

Brown rice syrup—A light and delicate natural sweetener made from brown rice and water. Used to sweeten dressings and dessert sauces, brown rice syrup has about 75% less natural sugar than honey or maple syrup. Over 50% of brown rice syrup is made up of complex sugars, which means the body has to break it down to a simple sugar before it penetrates the bloodstream. This helps to curve the sugar highs and lows that are common with refined sugar products.

Bulgur—Cracked wheat that has been hulled, parboiled, and dried. This nutty-flavored textured cereal is popular in taboulleh, pilaf, and kasha varnishkes. To cook, simply pour boiling water over the bulgur, cover, and let stand for about 15 minutes or until tender.

Carob—Carob comes from an evergreen tree whose pods are eaten both fresh and dried. It is high in protein and sugar and can be found in powder form or chips. There are unsweetened carob chips now available in natural foods stores.

Couscous—A Moroccan food made from semolina flour, a refined durum wheat. More nutritious types of couscous, higher in fiber (such as durum semolina couscous, or whole wheat couscous), are now available in natural foods stores. Couscous is typically steamed in the top of a two-part pot which has vegetables or meats cooking below.

Daikon—A large radish, off-white in color and longer and larger than a carrot or parsnip. Daikon is used extensively either raw or cooked in Japanese cooking.

Dulse—A nutritious sea vegetable that is purple-red in color and cooks up quickly. It can be used in any recipe calling for wakame, but it is much more fragile to handle. Dulse is one of the highest natural food sources of iron. It is also very rich in potassium, good for kidney function, and contains magnesium for RNA and DNA production.

Egg replacer—A powdered egg substitute used for replacing eggs in baking recipes and even crêpes. It is made primarily from potato starch and tapioca flour and is an animal-free product.

Fructose—The form of sugar found in many plants (especially fruit) and honey. It tastes sweeter than the sucrose found in refined sugar and contains half as many calories. It is not necessarily more healthful or natural than other forms of sugar, especially when crystallized.

FruitSource—A powdered form of white grapes and brown rice syrup crystals. It is used to sweeten foods and also acts as a fat replacer in baking.

Gluten—A protein substance found in certain flours, especially hard wheat. When moistened, gluten becomes tough and stretchy. It is responsible for making bread dough elastic and traps the air bubbles produced by yeast. Gluten flour or vital wheat gluten is pure gluten, all protein with no carbohydrates.

Hijiki—A strong-flavored sea vegetable, dark in color. Hijiki must be washed thoroughly to remove any grit. It can be delicious cooked with onions and tofu or used to compliment greens, soups, or salads.

Jicama—A root vegetable that is crispy and slightly sweet. It has a tan, flaky skin with white flesh. Jicama can be used raw, shredded, or julienned in salads or cooked as a vegetable side dish.

Kamut—Kamut is an ancient grain thought to be an ancestor of modern hybrid wheat. Like spelt, kamut was introduced in the U.S. so recently that the grain has not been included in the USDA's analysis. However, recent studies show kamut contains 20 to 40 percent more protein than common varieties of wheat. When cooked, its crunchy kernels are wonderful served as a pilaf or sprinkled over a tossed salad.

Kasha—Originating in Russia, this term is used for roasted buckwheat. It is flaky when cooked and heartier in flavor than buckwheat groats.

Kelp—A sea vegetable rich in natural iodine. Available in powdered form, kelp can be used as a salt substitute. In its dried form, kelp can be used in soups, stews, and vegetable dishes or baked or fried until crispy for a snack.

Kombu—Kombu is dried kelp. It can be found in strips or in flakes. Add kombu strips to soup stocks for flavor or to bean soups to improve flavor and digestion. Once it is cooked and has expanded, remove kombu from the stock, let cool, slice into strips, and return to the soup.

Kuzu—Kuzu is a concentrated starch from the kudzu plant. It can be found as powder or crystals and is used as a thickener, similar to arrowroot and cornstarch. In Japan it is used for medicinal purposes. In macrobiotic cooking, kuzu is referred to as a yang starch.

Mesclun—A mixture of young salad greens, often including wild chicory, mâche, curly escarole, dandelion, and radicchio.

Mesquite—A scrub tree that grows wild in the southwestern U.S. and Mexico. Using it to cook with adds smoked flavor to grilled food.

Miso—One of the oldest condiments known to man. Miso is a fermented paste made from beans and/or grains and salt. It contains 10 to 12% protein. Because it is a fermented food, it is a remarkable digestive aid. Miso can be used as a flavoring for soups, dressings, sauces, vegetables, and soy foods and comes in a wide variety of flavors and colors. Never boil miso, as very high heat will destroy its beneficial enzymes. When miso is added to a hot soup, try to consume it within 5 to 10 minutes to receive the maximum digestive benefits.

Nori—A high-protein red seaweed that is sometimes dyed. In the U.S. nori is used mostly as the paper-thin wrapper in which sushi is rolled. In Asian countries it is used as a condiment or as a main dish. Avoid buying nori sheets that are a uniform green. Choose those that are multi-hued in color.

Nutritional yeast—An excellent food supplement, nutritional yeast is very rich in B vitamins and protein, but low in calories. Nutritional yeast is composed of inactive microorganisms that are safe to eat without cooking. It has a cheese-like flavor.

Nutritional yeast is different from brewer's yeast, which has a very bitter flavor, and active or baking yeast, which would cause discomfort if eaten raw. Nutritional yeast can add flavor and nutrients as garnish over salads or as an ingredient in sauces and soups.

Orzo—A rice-shaped pasta popular in Italy and Greece.

Plantain—A fruit closely related to the banana, but whose higher starch and lower sugar content make it suitable for cooking. A native of central America, the plantain is usually larger than the banana and can be boiled, baked, fried, or used to thicken soups.

Polenta—A cornmeal pudding either eaten as porridge or cooled, sliced, and fried, grilled, or baked. Polenta is a specialty of Venice and northern Italy where it is held in special regard.

Quinoa—An ancient grain of the Americas, dating back to the Aztec Indians. Quinoa comes close to achieving a perfect balance of essential amino acids, the building blocks of protein. Its protein content is far higher than rice, corn, or barley, and it is high in lysine where most grains are low in this amino acid. Quinoa also has methionine and cystine, two amino acids that are low in most soybeans. Quinoa has been referred to as "the best source of protein in the vegetable kingdom" and is rich in vitamins, minerals, and fiber.

Rice milk—An important replacement for dairy milk products, made from brown rice. Rice milk is a little sweeter than skim milk and comes in a variety of flavors. It is also available fortified with calcium and Vitamin D to equal that found in dairy products.

Rice vinegar—This delicately flavored vinegar has about half the level of acid as cider vinegar. Brown rice vinegar is less of an irritant to the stomach than other vinegars. Rice vinegar can also be made from white rice and may contain additives.

Seitan—A meat substitute also referred to as "wheat meat." Seitan is made by rinsing or separating the protein from the starch and fiber of wheat, so it is fat-free. This wheat gluten protein can be cooked in a soy sauce-based broth, producing a texture similar to meat. Seitan can be sliced and flavored like deli-style products or cut into larger pieces for stews.

Shoyu—A naturally fermented soy sauce made from soy, salt, and wheat. It has a rich, complex flavor and is somewhat sweeter than tamari. It is more expensive than commercial soy sauce because of the aging required to process it and the superior quality of the ingredients used. Shoyu is best used in cold foods.

Soba—A buckwheat noodle prevalent in Asian cooking and available in Oriental and natural foods stores.

Soymilk—A cholesterol-free replacement for dairy milk. It has about the same amount of protein, one-third the fat, less calcium, and fifteen times as much iron as cow's milk, with far fewer contaminents. Soymilk comes in a multitude of delicious flavors such as malt, vanilla, carob, chocolate, and even cappuccino.

Spelt—An ancient grain recently introduced into the U.S. An ancestor of modern hybrid wheat, most spelt is grown in Ohio and lesser amounts in Michigan and Indiana. Because spelt contains gluten, spelt flour can totally replace whole wheat in baking breads. Spelt is about 30 percent higher in protein than wheat and can be found in natural foods stores in a variety of pastas or flour.

Sucanat—Short for "sugar cane natural," Sucanat is probably the highest quality granulated sweetener available. It is made by processing the juice from sugar cane. Sucanat is light in color like brown sugar, has a slight molasses flavor, and can be used in place of white sugar. Because it is not a fully refined product, Sucanat cannot be called sugar. It is also a rich source of potassium, calcium, magnesium, iron, and carbohydrates.

Tabbouleh—A Lebanese specialty mixing steamed bulgur with chopped tomatoes, onion, mint, parsley, lemon juice, and olive oil.

Tahini—Also known as sesame butter, tahini is made from ground sesame seeds. Very popular in Middle Eastern cuisine, tahini can be found in ethnic or natural foods stores. It has an overwhelming flavor which somewhat limits its use. Tahini is a good source of protein, is low in saturated fat, and is not hydrogenated. At times the oil may separate from the ground seeds. Do not pour off the oil; simply re-blend it into the ground seeds. The oil naturally protects against moisture loss in the ground seeds.

Tamari—Tamari is the liquid that rises to the top when making soybean miso. It is naturally fermented in vats for three months and in some varieties up to one year. Tamari withstands intense heat much better than shoyu, which is another soybean product.

Teff—An Ethiopian grain which has the distinction of being the smallest grain in the world. Rich in protein, iron, and minerals, teff has almost twenty times the calcium of wheat or barley. It can be found as teff flour, cereal, or in Ethiopian flatbread or instant seitan mixtures.

Tempeh—Tempeh is made from soybeans or a variety of grains ranging from brown rice to quinoa. It is infused with a bacteria culture that binds the soybeans and/or grains together. Tempeh has as much protein per serving as beef or chicken and 50 percent more than hamburger. Because it is a fermented product, tempeh is easy to digest. A four-ounce serving of tempeh has only 160 calories.

Textured soy protein—A meat substitute made from low-fat soy flour which is cooked under high pressure and shaped to resemble everything from ground beef to meat chunks. It has a high protein content, including health-promoting isoflavones. Textured soy is an economical dry product which can easily replace the texture of ground beef or turkey in sauces, soups, and stews.

Tofu—Tofu is the white curd made from coagulated soymilk. Probably the most popular soyfood today, tofu is rich in protein, easily digestible, and has been known to have many health benefits. For more information, consult pages 122-23.

Tomatillo—A Mexican green tomato that is small and pungent. It is not an unripe red tomato. Tomatillos are excellent raw, grilled, or roasted, then added to salsas or salads.

Umeboshi—Sour, immature plums that are fermented and salted with an herb known as shiso or beefsteak. The Japanese use it as a seasoning; others use it for medicinal purposes. Umeboshi vinegar has a fruity flavor, a cherry aroma, and a purplish color. Because it contains salt, it technically is not a vinegar, but is excellent in salad dressings to replace other vinegars and salt.

Wakame—The most popular seaweed in Japan, wakame can be found dried or fresh-packed with salt. To rehydrate dried wakame, place in warm water; when softened, gently remove and place on a cutting surface. Trim and remove the outer stem, and cut or chop the leaves for salads, miso soup, or to season vegetables or rice. Wakame has more minerals and nutritional value than most vegetables grown on land.

Wasabi—A plant often referred to as Japanese horseradish, whose root is used as a spice for sushi dishes. Pale green in color and very hot in flavor, wasabi comes fresh, powdered, or in a paste. Its intense spiciness has been known to cause a few tears to be shed when overused.

Yuca—A tubular vegetable, dark brown in color, with a white, starchy flesh. It is traditionally peeled, diced, and boiled and served with olive oil, salt, and pepper.

INDEX

ABOUT THE AUTHOR

At the age of fifteen, John Nowakowski started cooking in local restaurants and clubs in Baltimore, Md. The various cooking methods and food presentations fascinated him as he rose to the challenge of turning out dishes that were not only pleasing to the eye but a treat for the palette as well. The results were totally imaginative productions of contrasting textures and color. It was no surprise that by the age of 24, he became the youngest executive chef in the Marriott Corporation. From 1978 to 1989, John traveled the country troubleshooting and participating in the grand openings of award-winning Marriott Hotels. In 1986, he had the good fortune to train under Roger Verges at his highly renowned restaurant, Moulin de Mougins, in southern France.

In 1989, John joined hands with the Trusthouse Forte Corporation at Pi's Place Restaurant in Miami. It was there that a "Heart Healthy Menu" was created with exciting low-fat, low-sodium, and low-cholesterol menu items, using the freshest local products available. Pi's Place went on to win "The Best Restaurant Award" in downtown Miami for consecutive years.

At present, John is Executive Chef at the Regency House Natural Health Spa in Hallandale, Fla., constantly inventing and preparing new vegan dishes that delight the taste buds of devoted spa visitors who aspire to improve or maintain their health. John also gives vegetarian food demonstrations at the Whole Foods Market in Aventura, Fla.

John Nowakowski has also been featured in:
Dining In Miami by Barbara Seldin
Secrets of Great Miami Chefs by Surfside Publishing
Florida Chefs' Showcase with Julia Child
Vanidades Magazine and the *Miami Herald*

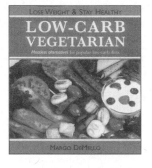
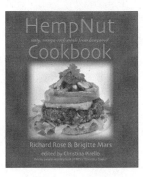